the **Scooter** book

First published in September 2004

British Library cataloguing-in-publication data:
A catalogue record for this book is available from
the British Library.

Published by Haynes Publishing,
Sparkford, Yeovil, Somerset BA22 7JJ, UK

Tel: 01963 442030 Fax: 01963 440001
Int. tel: +44 1963 442030 Fax: +44 1963 440001

E-mail: sales@haynes.co.uk
Website: www.haynes.co.uk

ISBN 1 84425 095 4

Library of Congress catalog card number 2004104457

Haynes North America Inc.
861 Lawrence Drive, Newbury Park, California 91320, USA

Designed by Simon Larkin
Printed and bound in Great Britain by
J. H. Haynes & Co Ltd

the Scooter book

Everything you need to know about owning, enjoying and maintaining your scooter

Alan Seeley

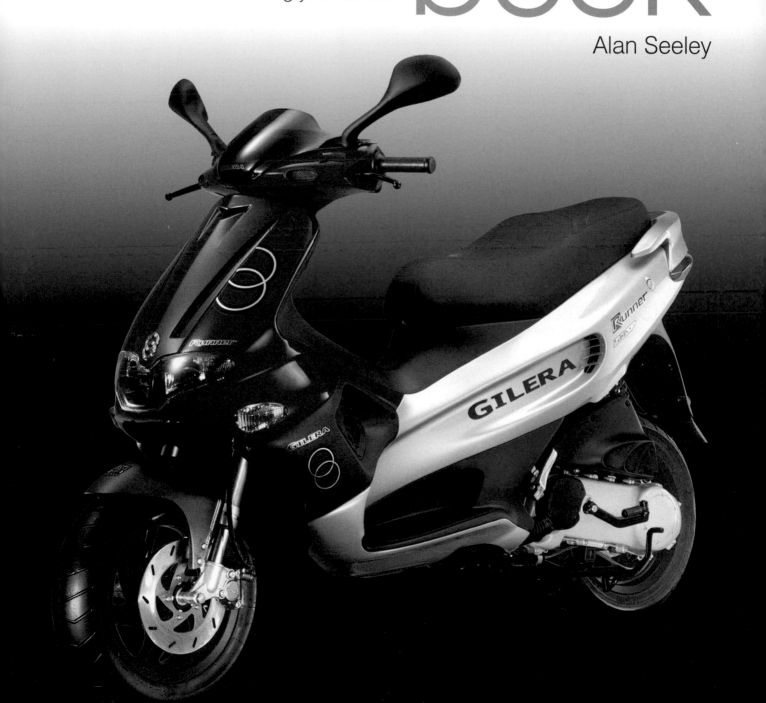

1
Which scooter?

Buying a scooter	10
Basic entry level 50cc scooters	12
Standard 50cc scooters	14
50cc sports scooters	16
50–120cc scooters	20
125cc scooters	22
Super scooters	26
Big-wheeled scooters	30
Electric scooters	32

2
Getting **on the road**

Test options	36
CBT	38
The theory test	40
The main test	41
Helmets	42
Jackets and trousers	44
Gloves	46
Footwear	48
Waterproofs	50
Thermals	52
Insurance	54
Security	56
Luggage and storage	60
Accessories	62

Know your scooter

Anatomy	**66**
Engine types	**68**
Fuel Systems	**72**
Ignition	**76**
Exhaust systems	**78**
Transmission	**80**
Electrics	**82**
Frames	**84**
Tyres	**86**
Suspension	**88**
Brakes	**90**
Bodywork	**92**
Derestriction and tuning	**94**

Looking after your scooter

Tools & maintenance	**104**
Cleaning	**108**
Daily pre-ride checks	**110**
Routine maintenance	**114**
Brakes	**126**
Cables	**130**
Bearings	**132**
Electrical	**134**
MoTs	**136**
Storage	**140**
Troubleshooting	**142**
Glossary	**152**
Index	**156**

1

Which scooter?

Buying a scooter	10
Basic entry level 50cc scooters	12
Standard 50cc scooters	14
50cc sports scooters	16
50–120cc scooters	20
125cc scooters	22
Super scooters	26
Big-wheeled scooters	30
Electric scooters	32

Which
scooter?

Scootering's recent popularity explosion is more than a mere renaissance. Everyone from the thrill-seeking teenager to the jaded commuter is realising the freedom and independence that the two-wheeled world's most practical machines have to offer.

If you were told you could slash your commuting times and transport bills, do your own small part for the environment and park up easily when you reached your destination, you'd be pretty interested, if a little sceptical.

But all of the above is true. A scooter can cut car commuting time by two-thirds or more, and eight can be parked in the space required by one car, usually for free. The whole experience is also rather more enjoyable than having your personal space invaded by strangers on a crowded train or your blood pressure pushed sky high in traffic jams.

Choked commuter routes, crowded public transport (and delays) and congestion charges – a reality in some towns already – are sending city types to the scooter showrooms in droves. Many commuters are finding that they can cover a week's travel for little more than the cost of a couple of days' congestion charge, and certainly for far less than the cost of a train or bus season ticket.

The scooter was born out of necessity in a post-World War Two Italy desperate for cheap transport. But the reliability and performance of modern machines have laid to rest the reputation of the oily putt-putts of old. Nowadays, 100mph performance is attainable on large super scooters. At the other end of the spectrum even a cheap restricted 50cc from one of the many factories in China or Korea will beat most cars or public transport across town.

Ease of riding is another key attraction of the scooter. With few exceptions today's scooters are automatic – no manual clutches or gearshifts to worry about. Anyone who is halfway competent on a pushbike can ride a scooter – the brake levers are even in the same place. 'Twist and go' they call it and that's exactly what you do. A twist of the right handlebar-mounted throttle grip and you're off. Some scooter manufacturers have even been thoughtful enough to link the brakes so you don't use too much of one or the other.

And did we mention fun? Where once teenagers saw scooters and mopeds as something they had to endure until they were old enough and affluent enough to drive a car; today's stylish sports scooters are fashion icons in their own right. There's no shortage of teenagers tearing up the tarmac on scooters long after they're old enough to be tearing around in hopped up hatchbacks with bellowing exhaust pipes.

A new generation of young people has discovered the pleasures of riding everywhere flat-out at 30mph – on a 50cc – or quite a bit more once the magic of derestriction has been worked and the joys of aftermarket performance parts explored. They used to say that scooters were little better than a bus pass – not nowadays.

In between the extremes of the time-strapped executive and the teenager going nowhere fast and loving every minute of it, lies a whole world of scootering. Its universal appeal can be seen in the sheer diversity of scooter riders: the busy student heading for her lecture; the shift worker for whom the scooter's convenience is without parallel; the elderly gent plotting a leisurely route from A to B; the proud customiser on a gleaming statement of his individuality. Scootering moves the world.

This book will help you choose the right scooter for you, get you on the road in the right equipment and help you get the most from your scooter. Freedom is pages away.

Peugeot Ludix basic transport at a low price

Gilera Runner available in a variety of capacities

Piaggio Liberty available in a variety of capacities on a retro trip

Yamaha Majesty go large with a superscoot, again in various capacities

Buying a scooter

Having decided that scootering is
for you, the next task is to choose
one to suit your needs, experience,
budget and driving licence.

Depending on where in the world you live, there
may be certain laws dictating how old you have to
be to ride a scooter on the road and the type of
training and licence you need. And then there may
be further restrictions on the size of scooter you
can ride and the amount of power it makes
depending on your age and experience. See pages
36-40 for the rules in your country. No matter which
class of scooter you opt for, there is a bewildering
array of choices. So before you sign on the dotted
line, here are some important issues to consider.

The high demand for scooters is good news for
prospective buyers. Dealers will often discount to
clinch a sale. Even where the manufacturer or
importer forbids discounting, canny dealers may
offer other incentives, such as free or discounted
clothing, accessories, finance, training and
insurance. In some cases manufacturers get in on
the act too, with finance deals, discounted
insurance and free breakdown recovery.

But be wary of on the road (OTR) charges. In
many cases the price listed, and no more, is what
you pay to get a machine on the road. This is
especially true of most European scooter
manufacturers. But some other makes allow
dealers to set separate charges for the pre-delivery
inspection, licence/number plates, road tax duty,
delivery, and even the fuel and oil the machine is
supplied with. And while they might not charge for
the air in the tyres, they could theoretically charge
for the time it takes the mechanic to pump them
up. So get all the costs and charges laid out in
black and white before committing to the deal. And
remember that everything is negotiable.

A further consideration is parts back up, both in
terms of price and availability. Most consumables
are generic items and, therefore, widely available –
bulbs, tyres, brake pads and the like. A budget
scooter from a country like Taiwan or Korea may be
cheap to buy initially, but what happens when parts
wear out or bodywork sustains damage? The
components may not be expensive, but they may
have to go onto a back order, which could keep
you off the road for weeks. So quiz the dealer
about parts back up, and price up some typical
items for the sake of comparison.

In some countries there are alternatives to
buying 'official' machines from manufacturer-
appointed dealers. 'Parallel' and 'grey' imports tend

to be cheaper than scooters from official dealers. A parallel import has the same specification as an official machine, but is brought into a particular country by importers that haven't been appointed by the manufacturers. They're then sold through dealers that are likewise not sanctioned by the manufacturer. Parallel importers can often source machines at prices lower than those charged to official importers, and these savings can be passed on to the end customer. The practice is legal, but the main pitfalls arise when it comes to servicing and warranties; many official dealers will refuse to touch parallels.

A grey import is a model not officially imported into a particular country. Again they are often cheaper than similar machines in their class, but on top of the problems with servicing and warranties, a grey import may not comply with construction and use regulations in the country to which it has been brought, for example in terms of important areas like lighting and emissions.

The popularity of scooters has led to dozens of new retailers springing up, many with little or no experience or understanding of the machines they're selling. Such outfits are often inexperienced in conducting pre-delivery inspections and safety checks, unlike established motorcycle and scooter dealers. You're less likely to find comprehensive servicing facilities and experienced staff at outlets where scooters are merely a sideline.

Of course scooters are reasonably simple machines, so fairly easy to make roadworthy and maintain. But they will usually have to be serviced by manufacturer/importer-approved dealers to comply with warranty conditions. In the event of warranty claims it is often easier to deal with an approved dealership for a large, established manufacturer. On the other hand, smaller players have most to lose in terms of customer satisfaction and, accordingly, sometimes they are more likely to give excellent customer service.

A further consideration when weighing up an apparent budget bargain against a scooter from a more expensive manufacturer is build quality. Will your brand new scooter start falling apart on the way out of the dealer's car park? Replacement parts for a budget scooter might be cheap, but if they have to be replaced more often than on a more expensive model, the cheaper scooter could soon prove to be a false economy.

Do some research. Read as many magazine reviews as you can about models in the class of scooter you're looking at. These won't say what a particular scooter's like to live with long term, but should at least give some idea of how a particular model stacks up against the competition. What's everyone else buying? Conduct your own straw poll of bike parking bays to see which scooters are popular – and also check which are standing up to the elements best.

Remember running costs – fuel, oil, tyres, insurance and road tax, and all the rest of it. The larger, heavier and more powerful a scooter, the more expensive it tends to be to run, repair and replace consumables. To maintain the validity of a warranty, manufacturers will often insist that only genuine parts are used, rather than cheaper pattern parts, which, in many cases, are as good as the originals. Regular servicing is a must to keep your scooter running right. Again, the warranty may state that this must be carried out by an official dealer.

Scootering is cheap, but shopping around and a little common sense will ensure maximum value for money.

Eeny, meeny… Choose your scooter wisely. As appealing though these three retros are, check out the whole showroom

Basic
entry level
50cc scooters

Many entry level scooters boast the same features as more expensive offerings. A number of European, Japanese, Taiwanese, Korean and Chinese manufacturers are very active in this sector. Names like Adly, CPI, Hyosung and Kymco, among others, are now familiar to scooter buyers.

Aprilia SR50 *once cutting edge, now little wedge*

Cheap labour means retail prices of scooters built in East Asia can be pared to the bone. This fact hasn't escaped the attention of importers and manufacturers elsewhere. The UK Italjet importer, for example, also brings in Taiwanese brand CPI, a high-specification brand that stands shoulder-to-shoulder on showroom floors with the more expensive Italjets.

There is also a degree of so-called 'badge-engineering', whereby one manufacturer makes machines for more than one importer, each of which markets the machines under different names. For example certain models from Taiwanese firm Her Chee are sold as Adly and Moto-Roma in the UK. Same scooters, different prices, although Moto-Roma models come with heated grips, useful on a scooter aimed at the British market.

Some entry level scooters from East Asia even borrow the designs of obsolete machines from more established Japanese and European manufacturers. Zhongyu's CommutaScoota 50, for example, bears more than a passing resemblance to Honda's Vision.

Another characteristic of the entry level sector is that last year's sports scooter is this year's commuter. With few exceptions, most modern budget scooters boast front disc brakes. A few years ago disc brakes were found only on the front of high-end scooters and motorcycles, while drum brakes front and rear hauled up lightweights. Some cheaper scooters, such as the Gilera Stalker and Kymco Super 9, even have rear discs.

The majority of budget 50cc scooters have two-stroke, air-cooled motors, while most four-strokes in the class are liquid-cooled. Two-stroke engines have long been favoured in lightweight scooters because they give good power for low capacity, are comparatively lightweight and cheaper to produce than their heavier, less power-efficient cube-for-cube four-stroke counterparts. But some manufacturers are finding it increasingly difficult to make two-stroke engines that meet ever more stringent emissions regulations. Some are having to fit catalytic converters, while others are building four-strokes. Liquid-cooled engines perform more consistently and efficiently than air-cooled motors, but they are more expensive to produce, and bring with them a whole range of ancillaries to consider like radiators, thermostats and coolant pumps. But as consumer expectations rise and emissions regulations get tougher, liquid-cooling will become standard, as it is on many sports scooters. Derbi's Atlantis is one example of a liquid-cooled, entry level scooter that almost defies its budget tag, putting many so-called sports scooters in the shade. For an example of the technological trickle-down effect, look no further than the liquid-cooled Aprilia SR50 – the original sports scooter – which was launched in 1994. Now superseded by the SR50 DiTech, the original SR is still a capable performer but now finds itself marketed at the budget end – good news for bargain hunters. Liquid-cooled scooters also tend to offer more potential for improved performance when derestricted than air-cooled machines.

Ah yes, derestriction. Performance is capped for many markets to make 50cc scooters legal for those countries' age and licence restrictions, officially limiting top speeds to no more than 30mph (48kph). True speeds can in fact be anything from just below 30mph to 45mph. In derestricted form a 50cc scooter can do anything from 45 to 50mph (72–80kph) and perhaps more. Remember that if you derestrict a scooter you may breach the terms of your licence and insurance. Road legality might be compromised too, as what is legally acceptable in terms of lighting and the like on a restricted scooter might not be up to the standards required for two-wheelers capable of travelling above the restricted speed. You might also invalidate your manufacturer's warranty, which is why most dealers are reluctant to take on derestriction work.

Peugeot Vivacity on a scooter this cheap, you'll be cheerful

Piaggio Zip 50 the popular choice of first time riders

Standard
50cc scooters

European and Japanese manufacturers are the strongest players in this sector, although East Asian companies are making inroads.

Yamaha Jog RR why did they call it the Jog when you can ride a lot faster?

Aprilia Mojito Custom
available as a 50 or 125, the Mojito is heavy on style

These 50cc scooters occupy the middle ground between budget utility machines and full-blown, teen-dream sports scooters. Paint schemes tend to be less overblown than sports scooters, the emphasis being on subtlety and style rather than impressing the opposite sex on the high street or down at the youth club. And some manufacturers are happy to experiment with retro styling to target the chic urban set – look at the funky, chromed Aprilia Mojito Custom. Then there's the Vespa ET2 and ET4 two- and four-strokes, respectively. Parent company Piaggio draws on Vespa's rich heritage by giving retro lines to its 50cc twist-and-go scooters. In fact the ET4 was the first ever 50cc four-stroke engine from a European manufacturer.

In this price band you can expect higher standards of finish and more refined features, such as better suspension. Some manufacturers offer improved security features, either as standard or as an optional extra. Leading the field is Peugeot with its Boa locks and immobilisers. Where additional security is an option, it makes good sense to take it, otherwise budget for your own security measures. It's money well spent as there are some models in this class that are as popular with thieves as they are with riders.

Further up the class and correspondingly more expensive is the Peugeot Elystar, which has a linked braking system that ensures the rear will lock before the front, letting the inexperienced rider gauge how hard they can brake without losing it. The Elystar scooter also boasts a low-emission, direct injection two-stroke engine.

As with the budget 50cc sector, air-cooled two-stroke engines are the manufacturers' powerplants of choice. The Beta Eikon 50, a liquid-cooled two-stroke, is a trick Italian scooter with sporty low-profile 13in tyres and a Paioli gas shock. There's also the Yamaha Jog RR, a slightly more expensive variant of the air-cooled R.

Some models are easier and cheaper to derestrict than others, and derestriction can also be more effective on certain models.

There's an element of badge-engineering in this class, too. Yamaha owns French firm MBK, which produces scooters badged with either name for different markets. Examples include the Yamaha YN50 Neos and MBK Ovetto, which are identical other than their badges. There's no denying the European influence on the styling but, confusingly, both makes are sometimes sold in the same country through different dealerships.

Again there's a trickle-down effect, as cutting-edge models are superseded. A good example is the Honda SFX, which has made way in the sports scooter class for the X8R.

Once you get away from obscure budget scooters, you can take reassurance from the fact that you are for the most part buying an established name that won't disappear before your scooter's had its first service.

What you are guaranteed with a standard 50 is easy, economical, reliable transport with understated styling. Another advantage is that they're reasonably easy to sell on, as prospective buyers will not expect them to have been owned, used and abused by boy racers.

50cc sports scooters

When manufacturers realised they could market 50cc mopeds to people other than grannies and vicars, the scooter revival began in earnest. Key to the revived fortunes of the diminutive two-wheeler was the 50cc sports scooter.

Back in the 1970s the more desirable 50s tended to take their styling cues from motorcycles, which riders were expected to graduate to after they'd cut their biking teeth on a moped. But the varying fortunes of the motorcycle market through the 1980s found fewer young people taking to two wheels in many countries.

What the market needed was a shot in the arm to tempt younger people back onto two wheels, even if it was only till they were old enough to drive a car.

Enter the sports scooter in the early 1990s, a machine you wouldn't be ashamed of if your mates saw you on it. In fact if your mate decided to get one too, a whole wider world opened up – a world of racing flat-out everywhere, the freedom to go where you wanted to when you wanted to, and an undeniable statement of cool.

The leading players In the sports scooter market are based in Europe, in particular in Italy, although a number of East Asian firms are beginning to get a foot in the door. In Italy scooters are viewed almost as a birthright for the youth of a nation where nearly three-quarters of a million scooters are sold every year. Italians carry their passion for all things two-wheeled from the cradle to the grave. As do the French and Spanish, who, along with the Italians, spearhead the sports scooter market. Aprilia, Benelli, Derbi, Italjet, Malaguti, Peugeot – these badges have become as important to the youth market as the logos that adorn their clothing.

Even the Japanese, long renowned for doing things their way, have put their hands up and realised that when it comes to sports scooters, they really don't know best. So Yamaha uses its wholly owned French subsidiary MBK to produce the classy but pricey YQ50 Aerox in standard and limited edition Toyota F1 colours. Honda has the X8R-S and X8R-X, which were designed by the firm's European department in Italy. While Suzuki looks to the Spaniards to build its AY50 Katana scooters.

'Trickness' is king in the sports scooter market. Expect flashy finishes and front disc brakes; many also have a disc at the rear. Upside-down front forks and adjustable rear shocks give even more sporting credence. Some sports 50s lay further claim to racy aspirations with twin front disc brakes – Moto-Roma's GrandPrix 50 and Adly's Predator II are just two examples. Wheels tend to be large, 12 or 13in, with sporty, low-profile tyres. LCD speedos and LED lights, commonplace on modern motorcycles, are starting to feature on some sports scooters. It doesn't end there, Benelli's 491 RR has braided brake hoses while Peugeot's Jet Force 50 SBC (synchro braking concept) gets linked brakes.

Peugeot Speedfight 250cc Peugeot's best seller

MBK Stunt (Yamaha Slider) enjoy the look on the cheap

Italjet 50 Dragster if you can look this good at 30mph, why go faster?

Many sports scooters are liquid-cooled, which makes them more tunable than their air-cooled counterparts. No wonder there are race series springing up all over for sports scooters. Some models are offered in air- and liquid-cooled form, such as Peugeot's Speedfight 2X and 2XP, and Italjet's Formula 50 and Formula 50LC.

There are no four-stroke engines in the sports scooter class. A two-stroke motor gives easier power and less weight, and manufacturers are working hard to comply with emissions laws while still delivering acceptable levels of performance. Catalytic converters are common, although manufacturers have to get it right or performance suffers. Piaggio, for example, uses a two-stage cat with a secondary air system to keep things clean on its Hi-Per Pro 2 two-stroke motor, as used in the Zip SP. Yet other manufacturers are dabbling with fuel injection. Notable is Peugeot and Gilera with their direct injection, and Aprilia with its DiTech system, detailed in the section on two-stroke engines. Apart from lower emissions, systems like this promise better fuel and oil consumption, which is good news for everyone.

Trick suspension on sports scooters was mentioned earlier, and none is more trick than the single-sided swing-arm front suspension on Italjet's Formula and Dragster sports scooters, and on Peugeot's Speedfight range. These curious hub-centre steering systems echo a concept most notably tried on Elf GP racers, Yamaha's GTS1000 and Bimota's Tesi motorcycles a couple of decades ago. While hub-centre steering never caught on in conventional motorcycling, there's no denying that it works. It enables you to brake hard mid-corner without upsetting the machine and there is a marked improvement in ride quality over telescopic forks.

Gilera DNA50 dash shows as much or more than even a big bike's clocks

Owners of sports 50s are the most likely to derestrict their machines. Inspection of a 50 at standstill will reveal little evidence that tuning work has taken place, with the possible exception of a tell-tale sports/race exhaust. But if you buzz through a speed trap at 50mph (80kph) on a scooter that is only meant to be capable of around 30mph (48kph), expect eyebrows to be raised and books to be thrown. One of the trickiest sports scooters to derestrict is Aprilia's S50 DiTech. Full derestriction is a dealer-only job, and few dealers are likely to do it unless you can show that your licence allows you to ride a derestricted scooter.

At the other end of the spectrum some models respond well to a simple change of exhaust system, although it's also wise to pay attention to fuelling.

The desirability and attendant thief magnetism of sports scooters has led some manufacturers to pay more attention to security. Peugeot again scores highly here, as does Benelli, with their factory fitted immobilisers. Peugeot's Boa lock, standard on many of its models, is built-in under the taillight. Turn the key and unfurl the Boa lock around a convenient lamppost or similar, then connect the lock back to itself. Check what security comes as standard on the scooter you're thinking of buying, and either negotiate or budget for additional measures.

Manufacturers of sports scooters are increasingly switched on to what their customers want. This is reflected in the aggressive factory customisation of models like Peugeot's Speedfight Furious and Metal X2, and even more obvious in the plastic bodywork protectors of the MBK Stunt 50.

Aprilia S50 DiTech there's a lot of technology hiding under that Spiderman bodywork

Peugeot Boa Peugeot are more switched on to security issues than most, the French firm supply the Boa lock on many of their models

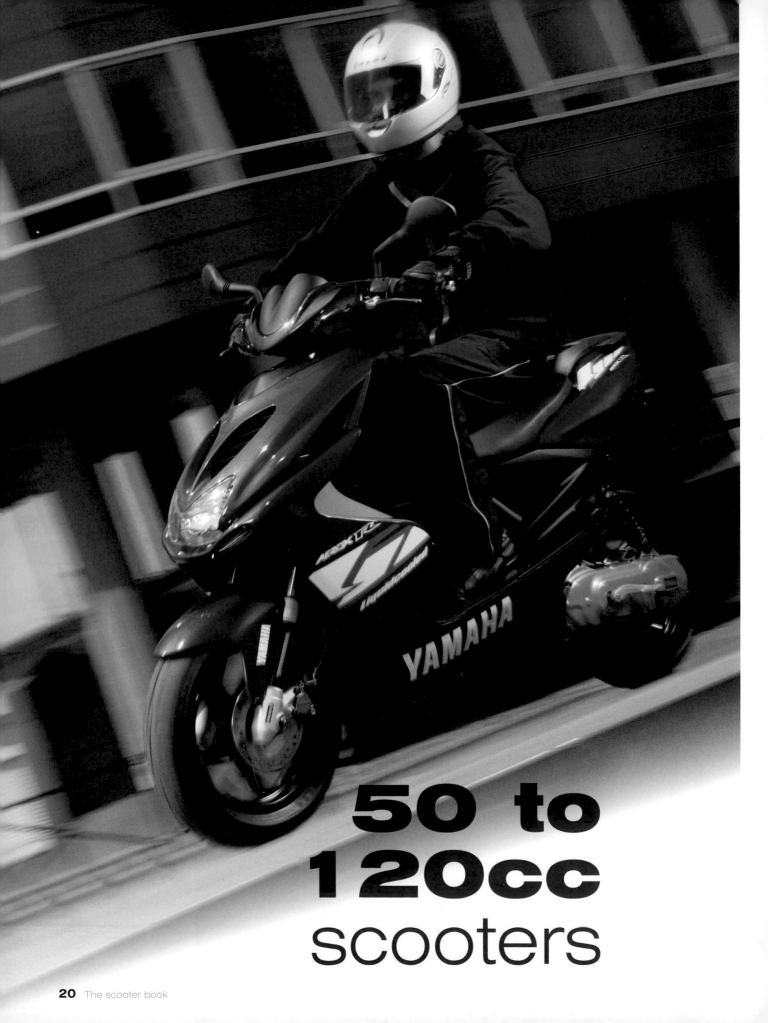

50 to 120cc scooters

This is the highest capacity scooter class where the two-stroke engine still reigns supreme. Anything above 120cc and current two-stroke technology is incapable of running cleanly enough to meet international emissions laws.

If your ambitions extend beyond commuting and running around town at modest speeds, and your licence permits, you might want to consider a scooter in the 50–120cc range. They can hold their own in faster moving traffic, which can be a daunting prospect on a slower 50cc model.

In most cases machines in this class are only a little more expensive than a 50cc scooter and larger ones offer a top speed of around 60mph (96kph), with little impact on fuel economy.

The best offerings come from European and Japanese manufacturers. But East Asian manufacturers, such as Adly, Hyosung, and Sym, are making sure they don't have it all their own way, despite struggling to compete on price.

This class offers something to suit most tastes. For something cheap and practical, the Indian-built Honda Lead SCV100 is a good bet. Drum brakes keep costs down at the expense of a little stopping power, but in any case you're unlikely to be blown away by the power from the air-cooled, four-stroke motor. Another practical option is Peugeot's Elyseo 100P, which is powered by a Honda-based two-stroke motor, but its lardy proportions compromise performance somewhat.

As elsewhere, Peugeot doesn't mess around in this middleweight scooter class. The company's 100cc, air-cooled version of the best-selling Speedfight comes in a variety of paint styles, from basic-but-stylish to the flashier X-Race and WRC 206, which marks Peugeot's success in the World Rally Championship. The bigger Speedfight also handles well. It has trick alloy footplates and a spoiler of debatable aerodynamic worth, but what the hell when it looks this good.

The more conservative Peugeot fan might prefer the more demure Vivacity 100 NP or sportier VSX 100P. All Peugeot's 100cc scooters are fitted with the firm's Boa lock concealed in the tail and immobiliser keys.

Competition comes in the shape of Derbi's Atlantis 100, Hyosung's EZ-100 and the Sym Jet Euro X100, with its Honda-designed two-stroke engine.

Sportier looking – and sometimes better performing – offerings include Yamaha's YQ100 Aerox, Benelli' K2 100 and Malaguti's Phantom 100 TD.

Peugeot Speedfight 100 plenty of build quality and features in scootering's middle ground

MBK Ovetto 100 (Yamaha Neos) a mix of styles in a budget price scooter

125cc scooters

Licence and insurance regulations in various countries have long made this an important scooter class. The 125cc motor is an ideal size for scooter engines. While still light and efficient, it can give the occasional turn of speed. A decent 125cc scooter is capable of 70mph (112kph) and many can reach that speed very quickly indeed.

Vespa PX125 classic lines and a real retro experience

With nearly 60 years of scooter building behind it and, as the true originator of the scooter back in 1946, it's only fitting that the Vespa name is still at the forefront of the market. The name is now owned by Piaggio, custodian of many famous Italian marques, and the PX125 is true to the roots of the scooter, with its two-stroke motor, pressed steel monocoque chassis and a sturdy yet stylish utilitarian air. Transmission is manual rather than automatic. What would normally be the rear brake lever on an automatic is the clutch lever, and the four speeds are selected by rotating the left-hand handlebar grip. There's also an optional spare wheel, which at one time was almost standard on scooters. A welcome, modern concession on the PX125 is its hydraulic front brake.

There is still the odd conventional Vespa-style scooter available. The Bajaj Classic SL125 started out as a PX produced under licence in India. It's relatively cheap and comes with electric start and a spare wheel, although the front brake is drum. Along similar lines is the LML Star Deluxe 125, but with a hydraulic front brake, although performance is let down by carb design to match the catalytic converter. Purchasers of either of these 'Indian Vespas' would do well to replace the original tyres with with some that give grip.

Everything else in the 125cc class is powered by four-stroke motors – emissions regs again.

Piaggio has brought the Vespa name into the 21st century with 125cc twist-and-go scooters that draw heavily on the recognisable Vespa style and construction. The pressed steel chassis of yore has more modern lines on the air-cooled ET4 and liquid-cooled GT125, but still offers excellent handling. The air-cooled model boasts a disc brake at the front while the liquid-cooled GT125 has discs at either end. It has 12in wheels as opposed to the ET4's 10in items. Both are capable of 60mph (96kph) thanks to the quick yet economical Piaggio four-stroke 'Leader' motor. The engine can also be found in the cheaper Piaggio Zip 125 and X9 125 Evolution, the 'baby' version of the X9 range of feet-forward super scooters. The Evolution comes with two front discs and a single rear disc on 14in wheels, all of which are linked.

Aprilia renamed its popular Habana retro-style scooter the Mojito Custom. This also has a Leader motor, as does the junior super scoot Aprilia Atlantic 125.

Benelli's Adiva 125 deserves a mention for its removable roof and is again powered by the Leader motor. Features include a low seat height and a handy 80 litres of luggage space. There's also an optional radio cassette player.

Beta looked to Taiwan for the Kymco four-stroke engine for its Eikon 125, while Benelli uses

Yamaha Majesty 125
*superscoot style with a
smaller engine*

Vespa ET4 *modern take on an old favourite*

Vespa Granturismo *touring on a scooter? Not impossible*

the 125cc Yamaha/Minarelli motor found in Yamaha's smallest Majesty, which is built in Spain. Malaguti's Madison uses the same engine.

In an attempt to make up some of the power deficit between four- and two-stroke engines, Aprilia opted for a liquid-cooled four-valve engine for its Leonardo 125 ST. It's pretty good, but with 139kg to push along, it has its work cut out.

The four-valve liquid-cooled version of Piaggio's Leader engine appears once more in the Gilera Runner VX 125. The machine is as powerful as the two-stroke it replaced and has twin shocks for improved handling and an engine immobiliser.

The Piaggio Skipper has the air-cooled version of the Leader motor, quality Showa forks and a capacious top box.

Honda has two Italian-built contenders in the 125cc class: the Dylan, which is aimed at the commuter market, and the fuel-injected, executive-style Pantheon FES.

Italjet has the Millennium super/maxi 125cc scooter and the curvy Jet Set, its lines apparently inspired by that hairdressers' favourite, the Audi TT motor car.

East Asian concerns are pretty busy when it comes to 125cc scooters. Chinese company Kangda has a variety of competitively priced, air-cooled four-strokes. These range from the budget ZS125T-3 with its 10in drum-braked wheels, through the T-4 disc and drum-braked, feet-forward soooter, the sporty T7 and the oddly styled T9. Also from China are Branson, Moto-Roma and Fosti.

Taiwanese firm Kymco produces Italian designs in its East Asian plants, and often steals a march on its local rivals with good build quality and handling. Kymco currently builds around half a million bikes and scooters a year and sells them in 44 countries on four continents.

Kymco's Movie XL125 is aimed squarely at scooters like Vespa's ET4, and aggressively undercuts on price. The Miler 125 caters for executives. It features good weather protection, a mobile phone socket, a digital clock and a courtesy light in the luggage bay. There's also the Ego 125, almost sporty in style but hefty and slow.

Yamaha's French wing, MBK, produces the Thunder 125 all-rounder, identical to Yamaha's Maxster, and the more staid Doodo 125, which is lighter and nippier than the Thunder. The Skyliner, essentially a 125cc Yamaha Majesty with a different badge, has a lower price tag.

Still in France, Peugeot offers two versions of the Elystar: the 125P, with linked ABS brakes and fuel injection; and the Elystar Advantage without those, er, advantages but a lower price tag. Then there's the fuel-injected, four-stroke Jet Force 125, which has linked brakes as standard and the option of a servo-assisted anti-lock brake system. A supercharged version is on the Peugeot drawing board. The frame is a motorcycle-style alloy dual beam.

Back in Taiwan, Sym makes the retro-style Euro MX 125, the stylish Megalo, executive Joyride with 40 litres of underseat storage space and the trick looking Shark, which boasts a rim-mounted front disc brake.

So plenty of choice in the 125 class, and the machines described above are by no means the complete list.

Aprilia Leonardo ST a work of art?

Why choose a super scooter over an ordinary motorcycle? You need a full motorcycle licence to ride the larger capacity ones and many are as expensive as equivalent capacity motorcycles with better performance. The answer lies in those favourite scooter watchwords – practicality and ease of use.

Aprilia Atlantic 500 big motor, big performance and comfortable to boot

Super scooters

Where you would struggle to fit a pack of sandwiches under the seat of most motorcycles, a super scooter's underseat storage will gladly swallow a full-face helmet or two. You also get weather protection from leg shields and generous screens come as standard on maxi models.

Add to that 100mph (160kph) plus performance from larger capacity models, and longer commutes and even a spot of touring become attainable. The super scooter rider can graduate from being the overtaken to the overtaker, while retaining the jam-busting agility of smaller scooters.

The twist-and-go nature of super scooters also makes them a breeze to ride. Where the motorcyclist is forced to make endless gear changes, keeping left hand and foot busy, the super scooterist just wafts along.

Super scooters are invariably four-strokes, although the large two-stroke motor might soon make a comeback, although not in the form of the smoky, gas-guzzling conservationists' nightmare of old. Aprilia is working on a large capacity version of the clean and efficient DiTech two-stroke engine, which should soon find its way into a super scooter.

These larger scooters tend to have bigger wheels for greater stability. None are bigger than the 16in (40.6cm) front and 14in (35.5cm) rear on Piaggio's 460cc fuel-injected, four-stroke B500.

Several manufacturers produce super scooters. The nature of the market means that equipment and accessory levels are often high. Busy

executives expect a certain amount of pampering and a corresponding level of gadgetry. But manufacturers realise that not everyone who rides a super scooter wants all the niceties, especially if they push prices up, so they offer options according to taste and budget. Many models, though, boast linked brakes, heated grips, and even computerised reminders of service intervals as standard.

Aprilia's Atlantic 500 is fairly representative of the class. Powered by a single cylinder, four-stroke, four-valve motor, which it shares with Piaggio's slightly more expensive X9, the heavy Atlantic can still get a useful shift on. It comes with a rev counter, diagnostic computer and a socket to recharge a mobile phone. Aprilia also offers 125cc and 200cc versions. The Piaggio X9 500 SL goes one better with a system that allows riders to listen to the radio, talk to their pillion, or

Piaggio X9 lends its engine to the Aprilia Atlantic opposite

Piaggio X9 dash tells you all you need to know and more

BMW C1 can be ridden without a helmet in many countries

Suzuki Bergman has earned the unkind nickname
'Burgerman'. Big it might be, but the 400 and 650cc versions
have got engines to match. This is the 650

chat on a mobile phone. It also has an ice warning system, heated grips, and an optional push-button operated electric stand. The 250cc version is almost as well-appointed as the 500.

As far as weather protection is concerned, BMW's C1 range goes the whole nine yards. A roll cage over the top of the machine carries the front screen, a small roof and a rear screen. The rider is strapped in and most European countries have been persuaded that this means the rider doesn't need a helmet. Available in 125cc and 175cc variants, there is also a 125cc in Williams BMW F1 colours and a 175cc, the 200 Executive, which comes with a pillion seat, phone bracket and locking glovebox. A host of other options are available for the Executive. Some critics suggest that the C1 has something of an identity crisis – a seat belt and roof are hardly typical features of a two-wheeler – but perhaps this is the machine of the future. It's economical, easy to park, comparatively green and, dare we say it, fun. Benelli is at it too with an up-and-over roof on its Adiva 150. Critics say it is more sensitive to side winds than the BMW, although a mighty 80 litres of storage space may offer some degree of practical compensation. The Adiva's roof is removable and its design gives the rider a little more protection from the rain than the BMW.

Malaguti's largest machine is the Madison 400 which has plenty of storage space, a trip computer, an ice warning system, a mobile phone

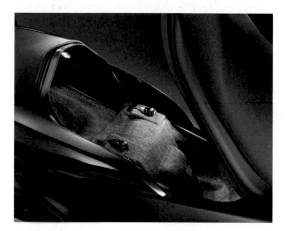

Yamaha Majesty 400 has a glovebox. Very handy

Yamaha Majesty's plush underseat storage

Yamaha Majesty 400 in all its glory

charger, and even a courtesy light under the seat. Linked disc brakes haul the thing up.

Gilera's 460cc Nexus, in common with some other scooters in the class, has its engine mounted in the frame rather than on the swing-arm. Big engines mounted on swing-arms do little for a machine's handling. Scooters with frame-mounted engines handle more like conventional motorcycles.

Suzuki's Bergman 400 is powered by the same single-cylinder engine as the Malaguti Madison, but its flagship super scooter is the Burgman 650 twin. Massive underseat storage space is augmented with three lockable compartments in the leg shields. The automatic transmission is electronically controlled, and has economy and power modes. A trick push-button selector is used to select from five preset gear ratios.

Yamaha's XP500 TMax was once the fastest super scooter on the market. Its 500cc twin-cylinder engine is another, like Gilera's Nexus, that departs from scooter convention by being mounted between the rider's feet for greater stability. Yamaha also produces the 125, 180 and 400cc Majesties and the VP300 Versity.

Honda can always be relied on to offer a quality machine in any two-wheeler class, and the Silverwing doesn't disappoint. The mid-engine layout aids stability, and as the lusty twin can easily top 100mph, linked brakes are a reassuring addition.

Super scooters are the luxury liners of the scootering world, as capable on the daily commute as they are on a two-week tour.

Big-wheeled
scooters

A few years ago the so-called 'big wheel' scooter was hailed as the saviour of straightforward, economical, twist-and-go, two-wheeled transport. Scooter critics have long considered the small wheels on conventional scoots as being what makes them unstable.

Scooter wheels can be as small as 10in (25.4cm); other typical sizes are 12in (30.5cm), 13in (33cm) and, occasionally, 14in (35.5cm). While the laws of physics dictate that larger diameter wheels improve stability, the weight and power of the typical scooter means that any compromises caused by wheel size are just that – compromises.

Nowadays, advances in tyre technology, driven by the burgeoning demand, means that scooter tyres aren't the simple sideline they once were for rubber manufacturers, who are working hard to meet the demand for grip and longevity, or a combination of the two.

The Italians were the quickest to adopt the big or 'tall'-wheel scooter. Styling may not be to the taste of scootering diehards, but the number of manufacturers in the sector suggests that there are plenty of buyers who forgive the big wheelers their quirky looks.

The typical big wheel scooter has a quirky mix of retro lines, and resembles a step-thru moped or anorexic motorcycle. While the tyres might be big in diameter at 16in (40.6cm), they're typically narrow in profile. Aside from straight line stability, those larger wheels allow you to bump up and down kerbs with relative impunity.

But the biggest sacrifice in practical terms is underseat luggage space. That large rear tyre means that there simply isn't the space for a locker to hold a helmet or two, a couple of bags of shopping or a sizeable briefcase. Some big-wheel scooters, such as the Rotax-engined, four-stroke Aprilia Scarabeo 125GT, make up for this with a factory supplied 90-litre top box and panniers. Otherwise you'll have to invest in a few bungee cords to secure modest parcels to the small luggage racks most seem to come equipped with, or budget for hard or soft luggage.

It should come as no surprise that most scooters in the sector come from Italy. Aprilia's Scarabeo is available in three versions: 50, 100 and the already mentioned 125cc model.

The Italjet Torpedo is available in two smaller forms, the 50 2T and the 50 4T. The 2T is a two-stroke and the 4T a four-stroke. The only difference between the machines is the engine. The 4T gets the economical, Piaggio-sourced four-stroke while the 2T gets the sluggish Morini-derived two-stroke. Italjet also offers a 125cc version of the Torpedo, which, despite being a four-stroke, is surprisingly sprightly.

Staying with the Italians, the plushly upholstered Benelli Pepe LX 50 can give the company's K2 Air sports scooter a run for its money in derestricted form, as it weighs 9kg less. One model that does offer a modicum of underseat storage is the Piaggio Liberty 50, a big hit in Italy and catching on elsewhere thanks in part to its budget price. Not exactly budget but well-specified is the liquid-cooled, four-stroke Piaggio B125, which comes with a four-valve cylinder head, digital read outs and computer gadgetry that put its technology right up there with many more expensive motorcycles.

Once again the Japanese have turned to Italy to design and build its 50cc big wheelers. Honda's budget two-strokes, the SGX50 Sky and more expensive SH50 (the delivery boys' favourite, and also available as a rather better-appointed four-stroke 125cc version) are both built there.

Flying the flag for France is the irrepressible Peugeot with its Looxor 50, also available in a TDSI (fuel-injected) version. The two-stroke Looxor 50 does not benefit from Peugeot's Boa lock or immobiliser. But the 100cc two-stroke Looxor weighs in with a factory fitted immobiliser and a disc brake at the rear, where the 50 has to make do with a drum. Same goes for the four-stroke Looxor 125 and 150cc SBC.

Love them or loathe them, the big wheelers have a strong following.

Aprilia Scarabeo shows the big wheel concept

Aprilia colour-matched topbox makes up for lost underseat capacity on a big wheeler

Electric
scooters

As 'green' as a scooter powered by an internal combustion engine may be, there's no getting away from the fact that they discharge harmful greenhouse gases and all the by-products of the combustion process. Perhaps, then, the future lies with electric vehicles.

Peugeot's Scoot'elec could be the future of green urban transport once battery range gets longer

There are already cars with both internal combustion engines and electric motors. Driving on open, fast roads the traditional engine charges cells that can then power the vehicle's electric motor when driving conditions are more stop/start and less demanding, such as in town.

Such combinations have yet to debut in the two-wheeled world. The bulk of a traditional engine, an electric motor and its attendant batteries make the proposition a little impractical for now, but electric-only scooters are already with us. There are of course the inevitable debates about the amount of energy and resources required to make batteries and the generation of the electricity required to charge them, but ignoring those arguments for the moment, the electric scooters that are already out there are emission-free. And there's one other pollutant they can't be accused of generating – noise.

It's still early days for the electric scooter. What hampers them most is the size of the batteries they use, their modest top speeds and limited range.

That said there's some fairly impressive technology out there. The Peugeot Scoot'elec can hum along at over 30mph (48kph), comparable with a restricted conventional 50cc scooter. Trouble is that its three colossal six-volt NiCad batteries offer a maximum range of 25 miles (40km). Availability will also be limited until such time as Peugeot has educated enough of its dealers in the specialist servicing the model requires. At 115kg the Scoot'elec is also around 30kg heavier than a comparable conventional 50cc scooter, so it would benefit from better

braking than its current front and rear drums.

Electric scooters are generally very low maintenance, with only the running gear requiring periodic attention, just as on any other scooter.

Fans of Italian style have a green option in the ScootElectric Oxygen, which is powered by a nickel zinc battery that can propel the scooter to 28mph (45kph) in economy mode, or 35mph (56kph) in what the company optimistically describes as 'sprint' mode. It takes five hours to recharge the battery; although 60 per cent capacity can be restored with a one-hour zap. As with the Peugeot, brakes are drum fore and aft. There's also the Lepton E from the same company, which can reach 28mph (45kph) and has a range of 20 miles (32km).

There are a variety of offerings from Taiwanese firms that bear the ScootElectric badge. A sportier looking variant, the Raider 45, comes with disc brakes front and rear and can hit 34mph (55kph) with a range of 25–30 miles (40–48km). There's also a ScootElectric trike that can hit 25mph (40kph) and will buzz along for 15–20 miles (24–32km). The retro-styled ScootElectric Magic has performance comparable with the Oxygen and benefits from a front disc brake, but it has only half the range and weighs 18kg more.

There are a handful of other electric scooter manufacturers; check the specialist press and local dealers for what else might be available. And remember, if you live in anything other than a ground floor flat, you'll have to invest in a very long mains electric extension cable.

Getting on the road

Test options	36
CBT	38
The theory test	40
The main test	41
Helmets	42
Jackets and trousers	44
Gloves	46
Footwear	48
Waterproofs	50
Thermals	52
Insurance	54
Security	56
Luggage and storage	60
Accessories	62

Test options?

Having decided you want a scooter, you'll need a licence before you take to the road. Current UK legislation provides a tiered route to two-wheeler licences based on your age, and whether you want a licence to ride any machine, including big bikes and super scooters, a 125cc model for commuting or a moped.

One difficulty with the current range of new scooters available to UK riders is that there are no models with fully manual transmission that are powerful enough to take the Direct and Accelerated Access test options (see below). This limits your options, unless you're 16 years old or simply want to ride a moped. You can either get an A1 Licence and stick with 125cc scoots of 14.6bhp or less or take a Restricted Licence on a machine with manual transmission, such as Piaggio's Vespa PX125, the only new scooter that currently qualifies, and then move to something larger after two years. Another option is to take a Restricted Licence on an automatic and move to a larger automatic after two years. As with a car licence, you won't qualify to operate manual machinery if you passed your test on an automatic.

The best route for those that qualify (over 21s and those that reach that age within two years of passing their Accelerated Access) is to do a Direct/Accelerated Access course on a conventional motorcycle. This will give you the freedom to choose which scooter, or motorcycle, you want to ride.

Moped licence

Riders aged 16 and over can apply for a moped licence. A moped is defined as a bike or scooter with a maximum design speed of not more than 30mph that weighs less than 250kg and has an engine capacity of 50cc or less. If it was first used before 1 September 1977 it will be capable of being propelled by pedals.

First apply for a provisional licence; forms are available from the Post Office. Exceptions are holders of full car licences who passed their tests before 1 February 2001. They can ride a moped without L-plates and do not have to take Compulsory Basic Training (CBT). If you passed your car test after that date and want to ride a moped, you will need to do a CBT (see page 38) before you can ride on the road. At this stage you must have L-plates. Then you have to pass the Theory Test (see page 40) before taking the moped test. Pass it and you can rip up your L-plates, and take to the road, with the option of taking a pillion along for a ride.

One loophole in the current legislation is that when 16 year olds who have passed their CBT turn 17, they can ride 125cc learner motorcycles on L-plates, despite having passed their test on an automatic.

Other licences

Would-be motorcycle licence holders over 17 will first require a provisional licence. Car licence holders automatically have provisional bike entitlement, but if you have no licence at all, you'll need to apply for a provisional bike licence. From 1st February 2001 newly qualified car drivers without full motorcycle licences have needed to pass CBT to validate their moped riding entitlement.

A provisional motorcycle licence entitles you to ride machines under 125cc with a power output of no more than 14.6bhp (which covers most 125cc scooters) with L-plates once you've passed your CBT. You won't be allowed to carry a pillion at this stage.

With a CBT under your belt, it's time to take the Theory Test. Remember that your CBT certificate and your Theory Test pass are only valid for two years and you'll have to retake both if you don't pass your full licence inside that time.

There are three types of licence: A1, Restricted Licence (A Licence) and Direct/Accelerated Access.

If your ambition extends no further than getting around on a little 125, you want an A1 licence. The route to this is the same as for a normal licence, but you take your test on a bike of 75–125cc and thereafter you're restricted to bikes of less than 125cc with a power output of no more than 14.6bhp. Again, that includes most small scooters.

The 'restricted' part of the A Licence concerns the power of the machine you'll be allowed to ride

for the two years after you have passed your test – no more than 33bhp or with a power-to-weight ratio of less than 0.21bhp/kg. Training schools can provide a list of machinery that meets these criteria, or it is possible to have a more powerful machine modified to bring its power output in line with the law. In the meantime you will learn on a bike with an engine of 120–125cc, a power output of 14.6bhp and capable of at least 100kph (62mph in the old money). Training for a Restricted Licence obviously goes beyond the rudimentary skills learned at CBT. Riders of any age who want to start out on less powerful machines can opt for a Restricted Licence, but under-21s have no choice.

Younger riders who reach the age of 21 within the two-year restricted period after passing their test can opt for Accelerated Access. This allows them to move up to scooters and motorcycles of unlimited power by passing a further test on a machine of 46.6bhp or more. But while learning on the larger machine it's back to L-plates accompanied by an instructor on the road (it's okay he doesn't sit on the bike with you, he rides his own), but you're still free to ride a sub-33bhp machine unaccompanied.

Anyone over 21 years-old can opt for Direct Access. As its name implies, this is the quickest route to a full licence and entitles the holder to ride a scooter or motorcycle of any power. You first take your CBT, either on a learner or larger machine. Once you've passed the CBT you can ride a learner machine on the road with L-plates. But you must be accompanied by an instructor on a larger bike, which should have a minimum power output of 46.6bhp.

Whichever training route you opt for, you will be able to hire the machine you ride from your riding school; many also loan riding gear. This means you can save making the financial commitment to a scooter and kit until you've passed your test and you're sure scootering's for you. But if you want to practice in the meantime you'll need your own kit and a scooter or motorcycle.

Honda SH50 is Italian built and very popular with pizza delivery riders. Not a bad choice of first scooter if a little bland

Compulsory **B**asic **T**raining

It means just what it says, but what does the CBT involve? Its main purpose is to provide you with the basic skills to ride safely as you embark on your riding career. The CBT was devised to reduce the accident rate among young and novice riders; statistics suggest it has had a positive impact.

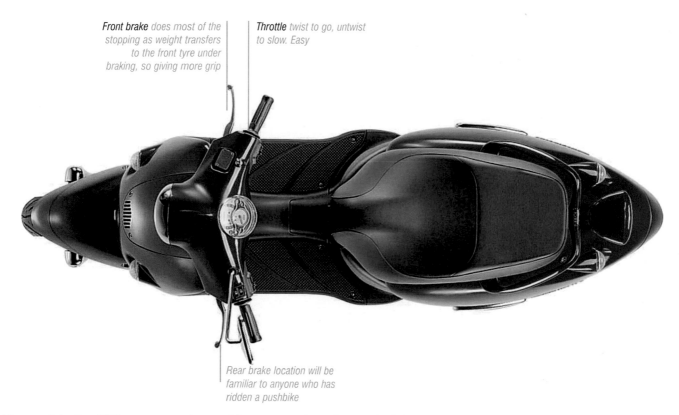

Front brake *does most of the stopping as weight transfers to the front tyre under braking, so giving more grip*

Throttle *twist to go, untwist to slow. Easy*

Rear brake location will be familiar to anyone who has ridden a pushbike

You can take the CBT on your own learner bike or moped, or hire one from your training school (see *Yellow Pages* for training schools in your area). If you don't have your own riding kit, gloves, helmets and waterproofs can be hired or loaned at most schools. Wear sturdy boots, a jacket (leather is best) and jeans in the absence of proper riding kit. The training school will provide you with a fetching dayglo bib.

Remember to take your licence with you. The instructor will want to check it's in order before training commences. The next formality is the eye test, where you'll be expected to read an ordinary car numberplate from 20.5 metres. If you usually wear glasses, you must wear them for this part of your CBT as well as the training and the eventual test.

By now you'll be itching to get on with the business of riding, but first it's into the classroom to look at what CBT involves and have a chat about clothing and riding equipment.

Then it's onto the training ground, where you'll be talked through the basics of your machine's controls. You'll also practice getting the bike off and on its main stand.

Now it's time to get down to the riding itself. You'll master starting the bike, pulling away, controlled braking and emergency stops, turning and U-turns. All this takes place in the safe confines of the training ground, usually a piece of hard standing a bit like a car park, marked out with cones and white lines. Your instructor will give all the tuition you need to grasp the various manoeuvres.

Just when you're itching to get out on the road to practise your new skills, it's back to the classroom for more instruction. This time you'll learn about riding and the law, the Highway Code, riding in traffic, anticipating other road users, and why you need to take more account of weather and road conditions on two wheels than you do in a car. It's all relevant, even to learner riders who have been driving cars for years.

Next you'll put all the theory racing round in your head and practical work on the training ground into practice on an accompanied road ride that lasts at least two hours. You'll be equipped with a radio through which your instructor will tell you what to do from his bike. You will work on road speed and positioning as you negotiate junctions and roundabouts, observations (in front and behind), signalling, manoeuvring and there'll be more emergency stop practice too. The route you ride will be designed to take in most everyday hazards and situations you'll encounter out on the road.

Back at the training centre, if the instructor's satisfied, you'll be issued with form DL196, your CBT pass. Now you're free to take to the road unaccompanied on a machine of up to 125cc or a 50cc moped with L-plates depending on which licence you're aiming for.

The CBT takes most riders a day, but don't be downhearted if it takes you longer. Everyone learns at a different rate; remember, your instructor wants to be sure that you're safe. A CBT certificate lasts for two years. If you don't pass your main test during that time, you'll have to take it again.

The **theory** test

With the CBT under your belt, the next thing you'll need to pass is your theory test, and that includes holders of car licences. The only learners exempt from the theory test are moped riders who obtained their licences by doing a two-part test.

To pass the theory test you'll need to answer 30 out of 35 questions correctly from a list of around 300. The questions encompass the meanings of various road signs, techniques and the theory of road safety. Various books have been published containing sample questions. The Driving Standards Authority (DSA) has published an official volume called *The Official Theory Test for Motorcyclists*. The whole process has been brought into the computer age too, with a CD-ROM available to help you learn your stuff.

You need to pass your theory test before proceeding to the main test, so do it as soon as you can. Like the CBT, a theory test pass expires after two years if you haven't passed your main test and you'll have to resit it.

In addition to the theory test there is also a hazard perception test. This involves 14 one-minute video clips that candidates have to respond to with actions such as change of speed or direction. The earlier a hazard is spotted, the higher the score.

The test contains 15 scoring hazards and there are five points available for each. The pass mark is 35 out of 75 for riders of two-wheelers.

The **main** test

Now you're ready for the big one. Time to put everything you've learned in your training under the scrutiny of a DSA examiner in a test that lasts up to 40 minutes.

Moped licence hopefuls will be on a 50cc machine; A1 Licence students on a 75–125cc machine; Restricted Licence candidates will take their test on a 120–125cc machine; and if you're going for a Direct or the second part of an Accelerated Licence you'll be riding a machine of over 46.6bhp.

Your instructor will have to accompany you to the test centre if you're sitting the test on a large bike. If everything goes to plan, he won't be legally required to accompany you on the way back.

The examiner will want to check your licence documents and your CBT and Theory Test passes – and you'll need some signed photo ID with you. This last item is required to discourage candidates from sending someone else along to sit the test for them. You'll be asked to do the same eye test you did when you sat the CBT (reading an ordinary car numberplate from 20.5 metres).

With the formalities out of the way, it's time to take to the road. You will be kitted out with a two-way radio like the ones used by the training school, so that the examiner can give you instructions.

The examiner will be looking for you to ride safely, sensibly and confidently, and there are certain things that the test must cover, regardless of whether it lasts the entire 40 minutes. You will have practised all of these at training level. There'll be a separate hill start if the route doesn't include a junction or set of lights on a hill, in which case you would have to perform a hill start in the ordinary course of events. You'll also have to set off safely at an angle from behind a parked vehicle. You will be expected to perform an emergency stop, under control and without locking up either or both wheels. You'll also have to do a U-turn and a slow ride with the examiner walking alongside. You have to match his pace to show you have good slow speed control.

Provided you manage to do the set elements of the test competently, and don't make any dangerous or potentially dangerous mistakes on the rest of the ride, you'll pass. Ritually rip up those L-plates. Congratulations.

You are not allowed to take a passenger until you've sent off your pass certificate and received your full licence.

But don't let your new two-wheel freedom go to your head. If you rack up six or more penalty points in your first two years of riding you'll lose your licence. You then have to repeat the theory and main tests. As much as you've enjoyed learning to ride, you don't really want to do it all again.

Helmets

Top of the clothing shopping list for any aspiring scooterist is a decent and appropriate helmet. As well as being a legal requirement in most countries, they make sound safety sense. Even at the modest speeds achievable on a restricted 50cc, a knock on the head can pack a considerable blow. That isn't scaremongering, it's a fact.

Modern helmets are designed to minimise damage to the head by absorbing as much of the impact as possible. A quality helmet that fits properly is a must – potentially it could save your life.

Many scooterists favour open-face designs, some for reasons of style, others for the excellent peripheral vision they offer over some full-face designs. This can be a real boon in the busy urban environments often encountered on daily commutes and during town work. Some form of eye protection is desirable, however. Goggles, clear wraparound spectacles or sunglasses (preferably not glass) on bright days all help protect your eyes from insects, dust and stones thrown up by vehicles in front of you. They also help to prevent eyes streaming with tears from windblast as you ride along. This can be a problem even on scooters with generous screens, particularly if the rider is tall.

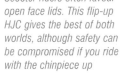

Scooter riders often favour open face lids. This flip-up HJC gives the best of both worlds, although safety can be compromised if you ride with the chinpiece up

Some open-face helmets come with integral visors that extend to the jaw line when the shield is shut. Others have separate visors secured with pop studs.

Some riders prefer the more enclosed and secure feel of a full-face helmet. With their visors and chin bars, full-face helmets offer good protection to the face and jaw as well as the eyes.

A helmet is no use unless it's adequately secured to your head. The chinstrap will be secured either by a pair of D-rings through which the strap passes, or a seatbelt style clasp. The advantage of the former is that every time you put your lid on, you can tighten the strap to a safe and comfortable point. With the seatbelt type the strap will have to be adjusted initially and then periodically to obtain the right fit.

The shell and the inner liner are the key protective components of a helmet. The outer shell is there to resist abrasion and prevent objects from penetrating in the event of an accident. Shells at the lower end of the market are usually injection-moulded polycarbonate, although this is sometimes found in some higher-specification helmets. More expensive helmets tend to use laminates of materials such as glassfibre, carbon fibre and Kevlar.

The inner is usually made from moulded polystyrene, and is intended to absorb the force of a blow. It does this by deforming on impact. Because of this it is prudent to replace a helmet that has been involved in an accident or dropped heavily. At the very least have your dealer send it to the manufacturer for inspection if either event occurs. Inside the inner is a foam-backed cloth, or sometimes leather, lining. This has no intrinsic protective value and is simply there for comfort.

Good fit is essential. Too small and a helmet will become very uncomfortable, distracting your attention from the task in hand. Too big and it won't give adequate protection. The correct fit should exert light pressure evenly over your head with no excessive pressure at any point. If there is

discomfort try another size or make of helmet, as liner shapes differ from brand to brand.

Some helmets, particularly full-face ones, have a number of vents to allow cool air in and warm air out, or to help reduce visor misting – difficult to avoid completely on full-face designs, particularly when the weather is cooler. Anti-mist preparations and laminate inner visors go some way to addressing the problem.

Take care of your helmet because one day it might have to take care of you. Never let it roll around the floor on its shell; always rest it on its neck aperture. Don't be tempted to stuff gloves and the like into it at the end of a ride. This can damage and deform the inner, so lessening its potential effectiveness, and Velcro tabs on gloves can make short work of soft cloth liners.

Only use mild detergents and polishes for cleaning as solvents can attack shells, inners and visors. Never buy a second-hand helmet as you have no way of knowing its history. And always wear earplugs – even the snuggest fitting helmet can't completely eliminate road and wind noise, which could damage hearing.

Whatever style of helmet you opt for, and some are aimed specifically at the scooter rider, a decent helmet with a good standard of protection and comfort needn't break the bank.

In many countries, and certainly in Europe, cheap and expensive helmets alike have to comply with certain baseline standards before they can be legally sold for road use. The current European standard is the ECE22-05, which you should find on a label on the chinstrap. Some manufacturers also flag it up on the back of the shell.

Replace your helmet every four to five years, even if you have looked after it, as the materials it is made from degrade over time. For this reason it's a good idea to check the date of manufacture, which you can usually find on a sticker attached to the inner under the lining. Scratched visors should be replaced as soon as possible.

Jackets and trousers

Clothing specifically aimed at the scooter rider is more widely available than it used to be and provides a stylish alternative to full-on motorcycle clothing. Many high-tech man-made materials that are extremely protective in terms of abrasion, impact and weather resistance are now widely used in clothing for riders of two-wheelers.

But when it comes to crash protection, particularly from abrasion, there's still nothing to beat good old-fashioned leather, especially leather jackets and trousers with built in state-of-the-art armour. Leather might provide the ultimate in crash protection, but other than wind protection, it struggles to keep the rest of the elements out. Here fabric jackets and trousers come into their own, and modern materials and armour mean they can run leathers a close second when things go pear-shaped.

Most modern jackets and trousers have a waterproof membrane under the outer – look for Gore-Tex and Sympatex labels. These fabrics keep moisture out while allowing sweat to escape – clever stuff.

What the clothing costs isn't always an indication of how water/wind/crash-proof it will be, but features like armour, and thermal and waterproof linings made of space-age materials, pockets and vents all tend to drive prices up.

Most scooter riders opt for a jacket in man-made materials, or a mixture of synthetics and leather, rather than 100 per cent hide. Impact areas like shoulders and elbows should have double layers. The next step up is to go for a two-piece suit where the jacket and trousers zip together at the waist – the further round your waist that the zip extends, the better the suit will hold together in the event of a tumble, and the more wind and water it will keep out.

Fit is all-important. Jacket sleeves must be long enough so they don't ride up when your arms are outstretched; likewise the back when you reach out to the handlebars. The same goes for trouser legs. If you expect to wear your jacket over winter layers it needs to be roomy, but not so baggy that it flaps around when you remove the thermal liner on warmer days. Adjustable straps at collar, waist, wrists, elbows and ankles help ensure the best fit. Flaps over zips help keep wind and water out.

Double stitching and extra layers are definite bonuses on impact points like your elbows and posterior. Fabrics lack the durability of leather, so it's pretty much a foregone that they will hole even in low-speed spills.

It pays to have decent armour at impact points – shoulders, elbows, and the back on jackets; hips and knees on trousers. Some cheap riding gear (and even some more expensive stuff)

comes with foam padding in these areas. That's not going to help much in a crash. Proper armour, designed to absorb some of the energy of an impact, will.

Armour is usually made of two or more materials. A harder outer made of dense foam or plastic, and a softer inner. The outer layer spreads the load across the inner layer, which cushions the impact. Decent armour treads the middle ground between too hard, which only serves to deflect the shock of impact directly to your body, and too soft, which has the same effect.

The importance of fit applies to armour, too. Make sure when you try a jacket or trousers on that the armour isn't free to move around and stays close to the areas it's intended to protect. If it doesn't, it won't be much use in a crash.

If your jacket and trousers get wet, let them dry out naturally, otherwise the material and stitching can weaken. Should they become dirty, clean them with a mild detergent solution and allow them to dry naturally. Some can be dry cleaned or the outers – less armour and liner – machine washed. Check the label. If your chosen suit or jacket is only showerproof, carry waterproofs with you to wear over the top when the heavens open. Most scooters afford reasonable weather protection to the lower half of the body, but not that much.

While decent fabric clothing should keep you warm and dry, it won't provide the ultimate in crash protection. But it's certainly better than simple nylon waterproofs.

Fabric suit (left) is a popular choice for many riders. Many offer a good level of waterproofing and effective body armour

Leather two-piece (right) affords more protection. Many now use a variety of fabrics in non-impact areas

Images courtesy of Frank Thomas

Gloves

There appear to be plenty of
scooterists, especially in summer,
who don't think gloves are a good
idea at all – bad idea.

When you fall, consider which part of your anatomy hits the ground first (if you have time to react). That's right, your hands. The reaction is instinctive.

Gloves don't fall under the banner of protective clothing for nothing. Once you've equipped yourself with a decent helmet, proper gloves are your next most essential line of defence.

So while conceding that you might not want the full-on functionality of a carbon-fibre, Kevlar and kangaroo skin motorcycle race glove, you want to consider something more than the fleece-lined soft leather numbers your great aunt bought you for Christmas last year.

At the most basic level, you must still be able to feel the controls through the protective layers of your gloves. Leather is great for this. It breaks-in nicely and moulds to the shape of your hands and their movement. Double layer leather and stitched-in protection should be included at impact points – your palms and knuckles. As with most clothing for two-wheeler riders, high-tech materials, such as Kevlar, Cordura and Thinsulate, variously for protection, weatherproofing and insulation, are increasingly common. The latter two are important because cold hands can't work controls properly. It's all too easy to end up grabbing too much – or too little – brakes and throttle. Many modern gloves combine leather with high-tech fabrics, while some are made entirely from non-leather materials.

Look for Velcro wriststraps around and above the wrist. You should do these up tight enough so that the gloves will stay on your hands in the event of a tumble.

As the seasons change, so will your glove requirements. Summer gloves offer optimal feel, in their better made (and usually more expensive forms), great crash protection but poor rain and cold weather protection.

Water and windproof but breathable gloves are now available for all-weather riding, and insulated gloves keep out the chill on the coldest days.

If your leather gloves do get wet, let them dry naturally, not on top of a radiator or in the airing cupboard.

When buying gloves it's a good idea to take along your jacket to check for fit over or under the cuffs.

Remember, never ride without gloves, even on the hottest summer's day. The gravel rash that can be inflicted by an otherwise innocuous fall, even from a 30mph (48kph) restricted moped, will take an age to heal. Smarts a bit, too.

Fabric gloves have leather palms. This is usually the first part of your body to hit the deck in a fall (Images courtesy of Frank Thomas)

Motorcycle leather gloves offer good all-round protection, but few are waterproof

All weather gloves are a useful compromise for the year-round commuter, and many have thermal linings and are waterproof

Footwear

With scooters being popular among commuters, many people ride in their work clothes, which could mean anything from navvies' boots, through handmade brogues to elegant court shoes for the ladies. Obviously the boots offer the most protection while the shoes offer very little at all. But neither protect your vulnerable ankles. Wear proper boots.

Given that most scooters offer plenty of storage and luggage space, there's no reason for not investing in more substantial footwear for riding and stashing your work shoes beneath the seat. You can then leave your riding boots in the space vacated by your working footwear (and the lock and chain you've just used to secure your scooter).

Boots are an important part of your protective clothing. They should protect your foot, ankle and, if possible, lower leg, which are particularly vulnerable in the event of an accident.

Leather is still the most common material used in boots suitable for scooter riding, but as with jackets, trousers and gloves, many modern high-tech fabrics are being used.

Motorcycle-style boots usually have impact protection in the shin, ankle, calf and heel areas. Foam provides the bare minimum of protection; look for boots with additional armour, such as that made from high-impact plastic. To prevent flexing in the event of a tumble, soles should be reinforced with metal or plastic inserts that still allow the sole to give when the wearer is walking. Zip closures are normally enclosed by a Velcro flap to reduce the chance of the zip opening in an impact and the boot flying off.

As a general rule, the more protective a boot is, the less comfortable it is to walk around in. That's not always the case, but you certainly wouldn't want to go rambling in a pair of motocross boots. Besides, these may look a little out of place on your typical scooter.

Motorcycle touring-style boots offer more of a compromise. They're usually a little more understated than garish motorcycle race boots and will tend to appeal more to the average scooter rider. Many offer good levels of protection with the bonus of some degree of waterproofing. Touring boots are usually pretty comfortable off the scooter, too.

Winter boots go even further by offering insulation. As with gloves, this is important for winter riding. Most of your body's heat is lost through the extremities. Apart from being uncomfortable it can result in reduced concentration or worse.

Most riders buy a couple of pairs of boots to suit the seasons.

When choosing boots take along the trousers you usually wear for riding to ensure they fit over or under the ankles according to your preference. It's also worth checking that your waterproofs slip over the boots reasonably easily, and that your oversuit's cuffs won't ride up as you're going along.

As with gloves, leather boots should always be allowed to dry naturally.

Motorcycle boots offer good lower leg protection. Buy a lightweight pair for summer and a thermal-lined pair for winter. Ladies boots (below, right) show that clothing manufacturers are getting more switched on to the needs of female riders

Waterproofs

While a scooter affords its rider a reasonable level of protection from the weather with leg-shields, screens and the like (and in the cases of the BMW C1 and Benelli Adiva an up-and-over roof), there's no getting away from the sideways or above-the-screen inclement weather.

Handy nylon one-piece waterproof (far left) comes with an integral bum-bag to carry it in until needed. Make sure you buy big enough to ensure freedom of movement, but not so big that they'll flap in the breeze

Two-piece suits can be bought big enough to go over your work clothes so that you arrive clean, dry and smart

Back in the bad old days, the dryness or not of scooterists depended on American army parkas (the iconic style of the 'Mod' scooter movement of the 1960s) or the waxed cotton jackets and trousers that were preferred by motorcyclists.

Both did a reasonable enough job, but required continual reproofing with waterproof potions or sprays, which made the garments permanently sticky and, as such, dirt magnets. Both are still available, but unless you're on some kind of retro trip, you may wish to consider something a bit more up-to-date.

PVC oversuits were the weather-beating revolution that followed waxed cotton and proofed nylon. They were certainly waterproof – until they ripped along their welded seams – but the build up of sweat on the inside, even on mild days, could make you as sodden as the rain you were trying to keep out.

Nylon is a popular material for waterproofs, and has the advantage of folding down small so that your over-garment can be carried easily, often in an integral bum bag.

Nowadays modern synthetics mean

manufacturers can make oversuits that are both waterproof and breathable – a real bonus on warm days or when riding for any distance. Many suits are lined for additional protection from the cold. Some feature reflective material to boost your visibility at night.

Check that seams are taped on the inside to stop water seeping through. Zips should have Velcro flaps to prevent water getting in through the closures. These closures should also open wide enough for you to get into the suit quickly at the side of the road. Choose a suit large enough to go over your usual riding gear; make sure it doesn't restrict your movement once on, but that it's not so big that it flaps around on the move like a gigantic sail. Velcro ankle, wrist and neck closures help to fit the suit to your body and prevent water entering in these key areas.

Waterproof overboots and gloves are also available and are worth carrying if you're likely to get caught out by the weather while wearing your summer gear. They fold down small enough to take up next to no room in your scooter's generous storage space.

Hardly the most glamorous of topics, but don't turn the page too quickly. You may have escaped the sweaty hell of overcrowded public transport for the freedom of your scooter, but be assured that cold can be a major problem.

Thermals

Cold weather is one of the scooter rider's biggest enemies. Your concentration can wander; your command over your brake and throttle controls is less accurate, which means accidents can happen easier than they might otherwise. Even when the weather's a few degrees above zero, the wind chill factor can take the temperature well down below zero once on the move.

Riding in the cold can be downright miserable, and riding a scooter is meant to be fun as well as practical. But with the right gear, year-round riding needn't become a feat of endurance.

Thermal one-piece keeps you warm but can do little to contain the author's pot belly

Just make sure you take this beauty off before going into the bank

Face and neck protector

Tabard to cover neck and chest

Fingers get cold first without thermal gloves

Don't forget some decent thermal socks

Thermal fleece is something you'll be grateful for

Thermal trousers – forget style, it's keeping warm that counts. Thermals make a huge difference in cold weather

Good quality thermal underwear is available in most clothing chain stores at reasonable prices. More specialised thermals can be had from bike, skiing and outdoor shops.

Natural materials work well until they get wet, either from sweat or rain, when they tend to hold on to the moisture. That's when the cold can set in again. Silk is light and thin, and tends to work better than wool or cotton. Synthetic clothing, on the other hand, tends to let body heat build up and up, which can become uncomfortable. One other problem is that synthetics tend to cause worse abrasions than natural fabrics in the event of a tumble.

Manufacturers of specialist clothing know the problems faced by two-wheel riders and offer a variety of products to solve the perennial problem of maintaining the right body temperature. Some garments combine natural and synthetic materials. These allow you to keep warm or cool as required, wicking sweat away from the body in the process.

A thermal neck warmer is also useful on colder days, filling the gap between jacket collar and helmet. A thin thermal balaclava worn under your helmet is also beneficial. Thermal socks and inner gloves are indispensable for keeping your extremities warm.

Thermal clothing might just seem like another laborious layer of protection to struggle in and out of, but on cold rides, which always seem to take longer, you'll be glad you made the effort.

Insurance

Any scooter used or kept on public roads has to be insured. Without a current, valid certificate of insurance you won't be able to buy a tax disc. Even if you keep your scooter off the road, perhaps in winter, it makes good sense to cover your machine for theft – unless it's worth less than the cost of insuring it.

There are three main types of insurance cover: third party only; third party, fire and theft; and comprehensive. Premium costs rise in line with the level of cover you choose.

Third-party only is the basic legal minimum required to get you on the road. In the event of an accident that's your fault it covers injury to the other party/ies and damage to their vehicles or property. It does not cover injury or damage to your own person or your scooter. Fire and theft are not covered under a third-party only policy.

Third party, fire and theft offers broader cover. As well as covering third-party liabilities, if your scooter is destroyed by fire (not that they often combust, spontaneously or otherwise) then your insurers will pay out. More importantly you're covered against the theft of your scooter provided you meet the security conditions set out in your policy. These cover where the bike is kept, and what level of security must be used, for example,

alarms, locks and immobilisers. You are not covered for any damage to your scooter, helmet or other riding equipment if you are deemed to be at fault in an accident. To cover those contingencies you'll need comprehensive insurance, but even this level of cover doesn't go so far as to cover personal injury claims or loss of earnings where the accident is down to you.

Insurance companies consider a variety of factors in calculating your premium, or even to decide if they want to cover you at all. Your age, riding experience (how long you've held a licence of whatever type), occupation, address, some motoring convictions, previous claims, where the scooter will be kept, and of course the type of scooter, all have a bearing on how much you will be charged for cover.

The cost of insurance premiums tends to fall at the ages of 21, 25 and 35. A 16-year-old stunt double who has the latest sports scooter, no garage, a dangerous driving conviction, a provisional licence and who lives in an inner city is the least appealing to insurers. You'd find a 55-year-old parish priest, on the other hand, who lives out in the sticks, rides a 50cc bottom-of-the-range scooter, has a garage, and has held a clean licence for 35 years at the other end of the scale.

Of course most riders fall somewhere between these two extremes and there is plenty you can do to keep your premium to a minimum. It also pays to shop around. Insurance policies, apart from third-party only, have an 'excess', an initial amount of any claim that you agree to pay yourself. If you agree to pay a higher excess, your insurer will reduce the premium. Similarly you can reduce your premium by garaging your scooter, fitting an approved alarm or immobiliser, and using additional locks and security marking, such as Datatag or Alphadot. It's worth taking all the anti-theft precautions you can. Insurers often refuse theft cover to people who have had machines stolen.

No claims discount can make a huge difference to your premium – up to 50 per cent if you maintain a clean insurance record for five years.

Above all remember to play it straight with your insurer. If you make any major modifications to your scooter, such as derestricting it or fitting performance parts like big-bore kits, you must tell them. If you don't they could refuse to pay out on a claim – they keep a register of claims and investigate dubious claims.

Most important, make sure you can get insurance cover for the scooter you want before committing to buying it. If you can't, all is not lost. Go for a scooter in a lower insurance group that you can get cover for. Scooters are graded according to type, performance, and how attractive to thieves they are. One insurance company may list a scooter in a different group from another if it has had a particularly high or low number of claims on that particular model.

Some manufacturers offer discounted or even free insurance for a period as an incentive to buy their scooters. This can offer substantial savings. But be aware that your insurance costs might rise sharply when cover under a deal expires. In some cases, depending on your risk factors and where you live, it can be cheaper to make your own arrangements.

Bad: young, inner city, inexperienced, more expensive to insure   *Good: old, rural, experienced, more no-claims than nostril hair*

Security

Statistics on the theft of bikes, scooters and motorcycles make pretty scary reading in most countries. Few stolen scooters are ever recovered, and victims of theft invariably find that their insurance premiums go up.

U-locks and cables can often be stored under the seat

Getting heavy duty with big gauge chain and lock

The physical security of machines is not a high priority for most scooter manufacturers. Most scooters have a steering lock on the ignition barrel, but that's pretty much it. Steering locks will only deter the most casual of thieves.

Some manufacturers are waking up to the problem of theft, though. Peugeot offers a flexible lock and an engine immobiliser as standard equipment on many of its scooters, and at extra cost on others. Piaggio's four-stroke range features engine immobilisers while Honda and Suzuki both provide ignition key security systems.

For the most part, though, it's down to the rider to avoid becoming a statistic. If you're able to park your scooter where you can see it while you go about your business, all well and good, but this is rarely practical, so you'll need additional protection.

Always use a lock, no matter how short a time you're leaving your scooter for. If your scooter has a front disc brake, a disc lock is easy to carry and acts as a visible deterrent.

A U-lock is bulkier but will usually fit in a scooter's storage space. It provides a similar level of security, and passes around the scooter's fork leg and spokes to prevent it being wheeled away. Some are large enough, or come with a cable, to secure the scooter to another machine or an immovable object such as a lamppost.

The next step up the security ladder is a high-quality lock and chain that allows you to secure

the scooter to an immovable object – disc locks and immobilisers can't stop a scooter being lifted into a van. Again these can be stashed in the underseat luggage space, but don't let them rattle around against a spare helmet if you're carrying one. In the interests of safety don't be tempted to carry a lock and chain around your waist or over your shoulder.

When locking up, take care not to thread the chain through a part of the scooter that can be easily removed allowing the rest of it to be stolen. Don't leave so much slack in the chain that its links or the lock itself can reach the ground, where a thief could attack them with a hammer.

While an alarm should be enough to put off a casual thief, again it can't stop your scooter being lifted into a van. Neither can an immobiliser, but at least it stops it being ridden away. Many insurance companies insist you fit one of these electronic security devices as a condition of your cover. Even where their fitment is not a pre-condition, insurers usually offer a discount if you fit one that's on their approved list of alarms and immobilisers. And as they usually self-arm when you park your scooter up, you won't forget to do it. Sadly, though, most people ignore the screeches and bleeps of vehicle alarms these days unless they happen to be their own, so you should use some form of physical security too.

Where you park is as important as what you do once you've parked. Busy, well-lit areas are best –

even the most brazen thieves prefer a little privacy.

Be aware that thieves often follow their targets to see where they're going to park or where they live. Don't get paranoid, but if you suspect you're being tailed, there's no harm in going round the block one more time just to be sure.

If you're parking at work, arrange for you and a colleague to lock your machines together if possible. If enough of you ride to work your employers might agree to let you use part of a warehouse to park in, or fit ground anchors in the car park. Make the security guys aware of your scooter then at least they'll know if the person taking an interest in the machine isn't you.

Some local authorities have fitted anchors in bike bays. Use them whenever possible.

If your only option is to park outside, you might want to consider using a cover so your machine isn't on permanent display. The more weathered and worn-looking the cover is, the better. There could be any old junk under there.

All the advice on parking when you're out and about also applies at home if you don't have the luxury of a shed or garage. If you have a back garden, park your scooter there in preference to out front.

Obviously the safest place to keep your

scooter is in a secure shed or garage, and it may be a condition of your insurance that it's locked up at night. It's best to put your scooter away as soon as you get home, and don't spend ages warming it up outside your house before you go out. Maintenance and cleaning are best done out of view too'.

Fit a ground anchor in your shed or garage. Position it so it's difficult for a thief to access when the scooter's parked up and thread the chain through the swingarm and back wheel rather than through the front. Again, ensure the chain is taut enough to be clear of the floor and the lock is positioned so that it can't be pulled to the ground and smacked with a hammer.

Make your garage or shed doors secure. The popular up-and-over metal garage doors are easy to pop open. Fit extra deadlocks, but not to the extent of advertising the fact that there's something worth stealing in there. Additional locks are best fitted on the inside of the door where possible.

If your garage is adjacent to the house, and you have a domestic alarm system, consider extending it to the garage if it isn't covered already. If your garage or shed has electricity on the same ring as the house, you could use a

Same scooter, same lock, same location, but the scooter on the left is far more attractive to a thief. The lock is on the concrete which could easily be used as an 'anvil' to smash the lock with a hammer through one of the links. With the lock through the wheel and round the front suspension, it is much harder to attack the lock, and more difficult to remove the wheel as the front brake caliper would have to be unbolted too. Even better would be to wrap the chain around an immovable object as well

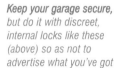

Keep your garage secure, but do it with discreet, internal locks like these (above) so as not to advertise what you've got

Security is getting smarter, but so are thieves

cheap baby monitor for extra peace of mind.

No one likes talking about scooter theft, but money spent on security is every bit as important as that spent on decent riding kit. Just ask anyone who's been unfortunate enough to lose a scooter to theft.

Remember the biggest threat of theft comes not from the casual thief or joyrider, but the professional thief, many of whom steal to order. Do what you can to put both out of business.

As many stolen scooters are broken up to be sold on as spares, there's one more security precaution that might put potential thieves off – marking systems such as Datatag and Alphadot. Tagging makes the rightful owner of stolen parts easier to trace. Unique marking numbers, microdots or microchip tags stamped on or fitted to various scooter components are recorded in a database that shows the name and address of the rightful owner. Police forces are equipped with scanners to read microchip tags, and tagging can provide the law with the evidence to convict thieves when stolen machines or parts are discovered.

If your scooter isn't tagged, you can buy a kit from your dealer and mark key components yourself, and place the sticker advertising you've done it prominently on the scooter.

If you buy a second-hand security marked scooter, the previous owner should be able to provide you with the documentation to register yourself with the company as the new owner.

Don't become a paranoid obsessive about security, but be aware. Do as much as you reasonably can to protect your machine. Above all use the best quality gear or ask the advice of your local police vehicle security unit and/or insurance company. With a little care and common sense, you can put scooter theft lower on your list of concerns.

Fit an alarm/imobiliser as a first-line deterrent

Most scooters have pretty generous luggage space. Underseat storage space and leg-shield lockers give you a place to store your helmet and gloves rather than carry them around with you.

Luggage
and storage

But there will always be those who need to carry more than the standard luggage space allows for. One option is to carry a large rucksack on your back. But in the event of a tumble these can cause injury or make injuries worse.

Where available, optional factory hard luggage is often the best choice. You can be confident that the racks that it mounts to will fit your machine easily and safely, and that the panniers and boxes can be supplied colour-matched to go with the rest of your scooter's finish. On the downside these can be expensive. Unless you can cut factory luggage in as part of the deal when you buy your scooter new, aftermarket kit is often cheaper and just as good.

Soft luggage is another option. Panniers are ideal for mounting over the rear of the seat. Many are expandable, waterproof to some extent, and

Yamaha Majesty has generous underseat storage capable of swallowing a couple of helmets. Or perhaps a load of shopping

Glove box with gloves in. There's a novelty. Handy cubby to the right is ideal for tucking away the all-important shades

Run out of on-scooter storage? Get a rucksack, but for safety's sake don't overload it with hard, heavy objects. Oxford pack (below) doubles as a tail pack, rucksack, or can be securely bungied in the footwell

they may even come with additional covers to keep even the severest downpour out. As far as fit goes, try before you buy to ensure that the luggage doesn't foul any moving parts or come into contact with hot exhaust pipes. Also make sure that they aren't going to compromise the comfort of you or your passenger.

There are also tailpacks available that mount conveniently to the rear part of the seat or on to the luggage racks fitted as standard on many scooters. These packs are again often expandable, waterproof, and many double as a rucksack off of the scooter. If your scooter lacks a luggage rack, there are plenty of companies making them. Usually these fit to the rear of the seat, but there are some available that mount to the front of the scooter.

There are two golden rules regarding luggage, both equally important. First, never overload luggage. Too much weight and weight poorly distributed might upset the handling of your scooter. The second rule is to ensure that luggage is correctly and safely secured. Follow the manufacturer's instructions and don't be afraid to

take the additional precaution of lashing things on with a few extra quality bungee cords or straps. They only take a few seconds to take off and on. Talking of bungee cords, make sure that the hooks fitted to the luggage's own straps are sufficiently strong that they won't bend straight under pressure, and that the hooks on any additional bungees you use are equally strong.

If your luggage carrying requirements are modest, a good quality cargo net or bungee straps is sufficient to hold small packages and objects on luggage racks.

A final thing to remember when it comes to luggage is to take care not to obscure lights or indicators.

One luggage manufacturer that has recognised the unique needs of the scooter rider is UK company Oxford Products. It produces a scooter bag that fits in the footwell. Apart from providing a useful 15 litres of luggage space over and above what your scooter has as standard, it features some handy external pockets and a transparent map pouch on top of the pack. Get it right and neither you nor your luggage need get lost again.

As with all gadgets and accessories, some are more useful than others. One low-cost essential is a decent tyre gauge. Correct tyre pressures are essential for safe and proper handling. The gauges on garage forecourt air lines are notoriously unreliable.

Accessories

Intercoms 'Hello, hello, are you there? Go ahead London. Did you see that guy? Are we there yet? Slow down. Speed up. Scream if you want to go faster.' Yes, intercoms are endless fun and make riding more sociable. And when the novelty pales, you can always unplug them

You may occasionally wish to converse with a pillion passenger. Bellowing at each other above the wind noise is the time-honoured method, but this can distract a rider's attention from the road. The solution is an intercom, available as an option or as standard on some of the super/maxi scoots described earlier. There is also a variety of standalone systems on the market.

There are even some that will allow you to communicate with your riding friends on other scooters, allowing the trading of insults and light-hearted banter to continue long beyond fuel and food stops.

A highly practical addition to whatever else you keep stashed in your scooter's storage compartments is a torch. Some scooters come with integral inspection lamps, but these will be of little assistance if the cause of any night time mechanical woes is a flat battery.

Hardier types who like to extend their scootering into the colder winter months might like to consider heated grips. Once again some scooter manufacturers offer these as standard equipment or as an option. Otherwise there are aftermarket systems that either replace your scooter's grips or fit over the existing ones. The better ones are designed to draw very small amounts of current, but check with your dealer or a competent mechanic that your scooter's charging system can cope with them, particularly if

Oxford mitts go over the handlebars to protect your hands from cold and rain. Great favourites of despatch riders and delivery boys

Tyre pressure gauge is essential to ensure correct inflation. Vital for safety and fuel economy

your machine is older or more basic. If there's any doubt as to whether heated grips will work on your scooter without overloading the electrical system, invest in a set of handlebar muffs of the type beloved of despatch riders. They know what works and what doesn't.

If your scooter is likely to spend long periods unused, invest in a trickle charger for the battery to keep it in tip-top condition during extended lay ups. For the price of a couple of batteries you can buy a device that will ensure you get more than one season out of a battery. You don't even have to remove the battery from the scooter provided the trickle charger's crocodile clips can get to its terminals. There are various makes of trickle charger on the market, but OptiMate was one of the first and has become something of an industry standard. Be aware that many trickle chargers are designed for 12 volt batteries, so if your scooter has a six volt system, ensure you buy either a dual voltage or six volt specific one.

Invest in a cover if your scooter has to be kept outdoors in all weathers. Not only will it protect your machine from the elements, it will also hide it from prying eyes.

Smaller scooters are often slower than other traffic on fast, busy roads, so it makes sense to be seen. Dayglo vests, jackets and belts all help to raise visibility, as do reflective stickers and strips attached to your scooter or sewn onto your clothing.

Heated grips are a luxury much beloved of the winter rider

If your scooter's going to be laid up for any length of time, and there's power in your shed, buy a trickle charger to keep your battery up to power. Otherwise it'll be dead and useless come springtime

3

Know your scooter

Anatomy	**66**
Engine types	**68**
Fuel Systems	**72**
Ignition	**76**
Exhaust systems	**78**
Transmission	**80**
Electrics	**82**
Frames	**84**
Tyres	**86**
Suspension	**88**
Brakes	**90**
Bodywork	**92**
Derestriction and tuning	**94**

Anatomy

Throttle

Brake lever

Grocery hook

Headlight

Front indicator

Footwell

Front mudguard

Fork stanchion

Fork slider

Reflector

Front brake caliper

Speedometer drive

Front brake disc

Dualseat

Pillion grab handle

Rear light

Rear indicator

NEO'S

Shock absorber

Silencer

Transmission cover

Rear brake actuating arm

Cooling fan

Kickstart lever

Stand

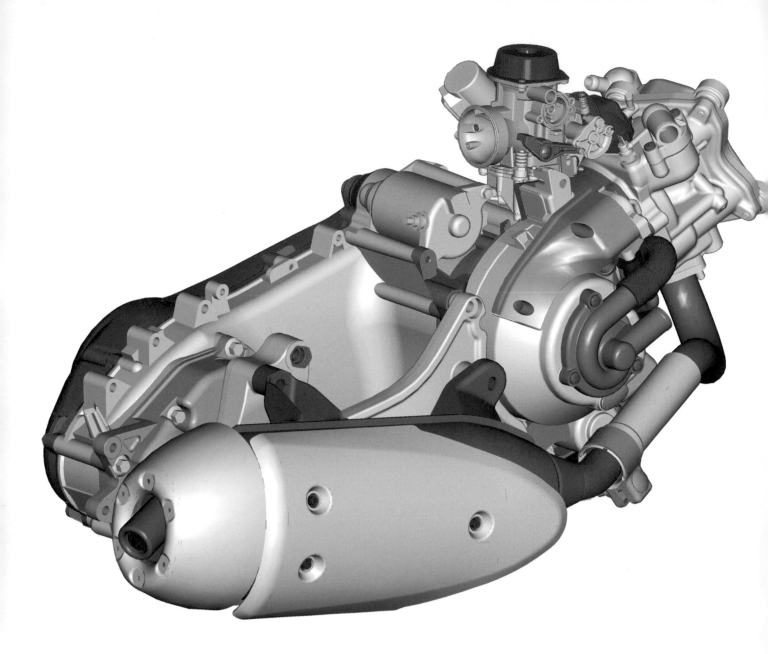

Engine types

When we looked at the different scooters currently available, it quickly became apparent that the two types of internal combustion engine used – two-stroke and four-stroke – found favour depending on the capacity of the scooter.

Smaller machines are predominantly two-stroke; the engine is comparatively cheap to produce, has fewer moving parts, and gives good power for its weight. Apart from the obvious benefits to scooter buyers of reasonable performance in an affordable package, manufacturers are keen on the two-stroke as well, because they are easier and cheaper to produce.

The two-stroke's problem is that it produces rather anti-social levels of emissions and is thirsty for fuel, especially in larger incarnations. In the section on fuel systems overleaf, you'll see an example of how one manufacturer is attempting to clean up the two-stroke's act for use in larger capacity scooters.

But for now it's easier to make four-stroke engines run cleaner for larger capacity applications, which is why they're found in virtually all new scooters of over 125cc.

So how do the two engine types work?

The strokes refer to the number of times the piston moves up and down the barrel for each combustion cycle.

For both two-stroke and four-stroke engines the basic combustion cycle is essentially the same. First comes induction (air/fuel in), followed by compression (air/fuel mixture squeezed), ignition (setting the mixture alight) and exhaust (getting the spent mixture out). Suck, squeeze, bang, blow is the easy, if slightly unscientific way of remembering it. There is a little more to it than that as we'll see in this, the ignition and the exhaust sections of this book.

But that, in a nutshell, is the process an engine has to go through in order to convert petrol's chemical energy into forward motion for our scooters.

There are a number of key differences between two- and four-stroke engines, but the most obvious is how they get the gases in and out of the combustion chamber.

Four-strokes

The four-stroke gets its name from the fact that it must complete one combustion cycle. At the start of the cycle the piston is at TDC (top dead centre – as far up the bore as it can go), and the inlet and exhaust valves are shut. As the crankshaft turns, the piston drops down the bore and the inlet valve opens allowing the fuel and air mixture into the cylinder.

When the piston reaches BDC (bottom dead centre – as far down the bore as possible), the inlet valve closes to prevent any more mixture entering the cylinder. That is the end of the induction stroke.

As the crankshaft continues to rotate it pushes the piston back up the bore towards TDC. Inlet and exhaust valves are shut to seal the cylinder; the air/fuel mixture has nowhere to go and becomes increasingly compressed as the piston heads towards TDC again. This is the end of the piston's second stroke – one down the bore and one back up – and the crankshaft has completed one revolution.

With the mixture squashed into the small space above the piston (the combustion chamber), it's ready to ignite. The spark plug is timed to spark at that point, firing the mixture, which causes it to expand rapidly and push forcibly on all surfaces. As the piston is the only thing that can move, the high pressure in the cylinder pushes the piston back down the bore until it reaches BDC and can't be pushed any further. This is the end of the ignition/power stroke.

Now the burnt gas from the cylinder has to be expelled. The exhaust valve opens and the high-pressure gas starts to make its way out of the exhaust valve and into the exhaust pipe. This is helped by the piston, which is again rising up the bore towards TDC, and driving the gas out of the cylinder.

Once it reaches TDC the exhaust valve closes

The four-stroke process in four easy steps; suck, squeeze, bang, blow. Also known as the Otto cycle

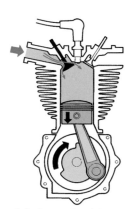

Induction: *as the piston descends the inlet valve opens, allowing the fuel/air mixture to be drawn directly into the combustion chamber*

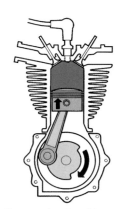

Compression: *the piston starts to ascend and the inlet valve closes. The mixture is compressed as the piston rises*

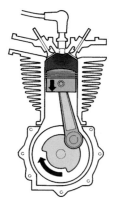

Ignition: *the spark plug ignites the compressed mixture, forcing the piston down the bore*

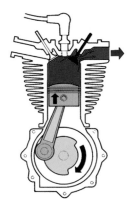

Exhaust: *the exhaust valve opens to allow the burnt gases to be expelled through the exhaust port as the piston rises*

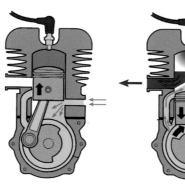

Induction of fresh mixture into crankcase and **compression** of existing mixture in combustion chamber

Ignition **and exhaust** of existing mixture in combustion chamber, and transfer of fresh mixture to combustion chamber

and the inlet valve opens ready to start the next combustion cycle. In all, the piston has moved in the bore four times (twice down and twice up) and the crankshaft has completed two rotations.

That's the basic operation of the four-stroke engine, but in practice the valves are timed so that the exhaust remains momentarily open while the inlet allows the fresh air/fuel charge in. This is because the escaping exhaust gas helps pull the fresh mixture into the cylinder.

Two-strokes

It takes a two-stroke half the time of a four-stroke to complete the combustion cycle. Unlike a four-stroke, a two-stroke doesn't have valves in the top of the combustion chamber. Instead, it uses holes known as ports in the cylinder wall, which are covered and uncovered by the piston as it rises and falls. By setting the ports at different levels, they are covered and uncovered at the appropriate times in the combustion cycle.

Another key difference of the two-stroke engine is that it carries its lubrication in the air/fuel mixture, rather than the re-circulated engine oil used in a four-stroke. A two-stroke's oil is either pumped into the crankcases from a separate tank to mix with the fuel and air in the correct proportion, or is premixed with the petrol in the fuel tank.

This mixture passes from the carburettor and is held in the crankcase, underneath the piston before it enters the cylinder. The oil content in the mixture lubricates the crankshaft and con-rod bearings, and the rise and fall of the piston is used to pump the air/fuel mixture into the cylinder.

With the piston at BDC both the inlet and exhaust ports are uncovered, and fresh mixture is displaced into the cylinder through the inlet port. As the piston rises it first covers the inlet port, stopping any more mixture from entering the cylinder and completing induction. As the piston rises further it also covers the exhaust port to seal the cylinder, and compression starts to take place.

The mixture is fully compressed when the piston reaches TDC, and in one movement the two-stroke has completed both induction and compression. A four-stroke's piston has to move

twice to do this. The spark plug now ignites the mixture and provides the power stroke. The piston is forced back down the bore by the expanding gas and the exhaust port is uncovered. The pressure of the burnt gas forces it into the exhaust pipe, completing both ignition/power and exhaust in one stroke.

In all the piston has gone up and down the bore once, but in the process has completed all four parts of the combustion process. The crankshaft has only rotated once too. As the piston travels a little further down the bore it uncovers the inlet port again, allowing fresh mixture to enter the cylinder.

At this point exhaust gas will still be flowing out through the exhaust port while fresh mixture enters the cylinder via a process known as scavenging. The main advantage of a two-stroke is that you get a power stroke for every crank revolution and there are fewer moving parts, which makes the engine cheaper and easier to build. The draw back is that they aren't as efficient or economical as four-strokes.

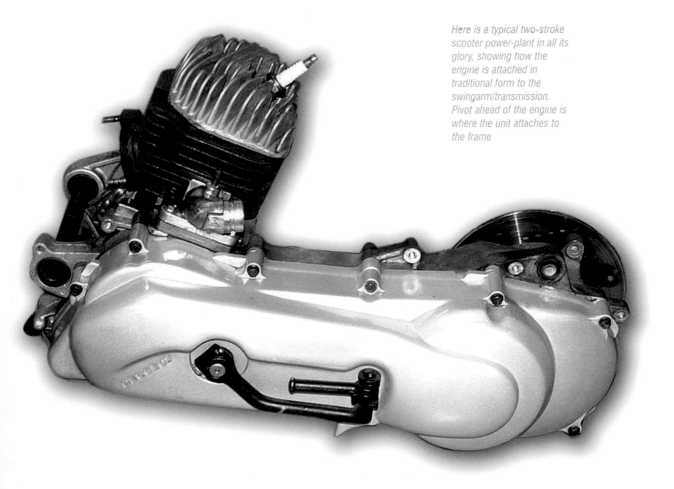

Here is a typical two-stroke scooter power-plant in all its glory, showing how the engine is attached in traditional form to the swingarm/transmission. Pivot ahead of the engine is where the unit attaches to the frame

A scooter needs to get fuel and air in to its engine in the correct amounts at the right time. The key concerns for an engine designer are efficiency, power and economy, and they have to work against a backdrop of increasingly stringent emissions regulations and consumer demand for good usable power with sensible fuel consumption.

Fuel systems

Slide carbs

Carburettors deliver the correct amounts of fuel and air to an engine for different loads and conditions. They do this using a principle called the venturi effect.

A venturi is a tube of varying diameter. It is a scooter's inlet tract between a carb mouth and the point the fuel/air enters the engine. In a parallel tube air can be pulled along at a constant pressure and velocity. Introduce a restriction by narrowing the tube at some point down its length and the air speeds up while its pressure drops. Where the restriction is at its tightest a slight vacuum is generated. Stick a jet linked to a fuel reservoir here, and the difference between the low pressure of the vacuum and the atmospheric pressure that the fuel's under cause it to rise up the jet and into the air stream generated by the engine's piston going down its barrel. To optimise flow the venturi opens up again after the narrowest point.

Fuel and air have to be delivered in the correct ratio, known as the Stoichiometric ratio, which is typically 14.7 parts of air to one of fuel depending on engine type. This figure might need to be as rich as 12:1 for maximum power, yet can be as lean as 18:1 for cruising.

So with the right size jets and carb diameter or 'choke' size to do this, there's just the small matter of getting the right amount of mixture in to vary the engine speed. With the slide closed in a standard slide carb a pilot jet provides enough fuel from the float bowl while a separate drilling in the mouth of the carb provides enough air for low speed running and idling. The throttle slide cutaway is there to smooth the transition between pilot and main fuel circuits between one-eighth and one-quarter throttle. It does this by emphasising the venturi effect. As the slide lifts more air can flow, the tapered needle opens up more of its jet and more fuel enters the air stream. The needle jet dictates running from one-quarter to three-quarters throttle opening. The main jet controls running from three-quarters to full throttle, the area of the needle jet now uncovered being greater than the size of the main jet, letting the main jet take over.

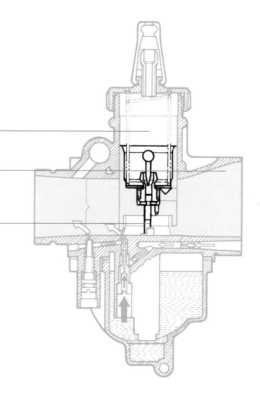

Slide Carburettor
Piston is directly controlled by the twist grip

Air pressure drops as the piston is lifted and more air flows

Needle the piston has a tapered needle attached which blocks the fuel flow. As it is lifted petrol is drawn up by the low pressure

CV carbs

A refinement of the slide carb described above is the CV (constant velocity) carb that can be found on many scooters. When the throttle is opened quickly from tickover on a slide carb, the engine can hesitate and even stall. This is because the volume of air in the carb is suddenly increased but it doesn't always have the velocity to draw sufficient fuel with it through the venturi.

A CV carb contains a piston similar to the slide in a slide carb. It carries the needle just like a slide but isn't connected directly to the twistgrip. Instead there is a butterfly valve after the piston that links to the twistgrip. The piston is mounted in a diaphragm; a closed chamber above it is linked to the venturi via an air passage or a hole in the bottom of the piston. The area below the diaphragm fills with air at atmospheric pressure. When the pressure drops in the venturi as the engine speed rises, as it does in the slide carb, the pressure also drops above the diaphragm, which starts to lift because there is air at higher (than atmospheric) pressure below it.

With a CV carb it doesn't matter how ham-fisted the rider is with the throttle. The piston fills the venturi until such time as the engine speed is fast enough to generate sufficient 'venturi effect' (i.e. low pressure from quick moving air) to lift the piston. This means that the venturi cannot suddenly fill with a large volume of near static air. The result is that the fuel/air mix can be much closer to the ideal at all times, which results in greater efficiency.

Constant velocity (CV) carburettor

Air is routed up into the vacuum chamber via a hole in the base of the piston

Air at atmospheric pressure fills the area below the diaphragm

Return spring helps to stabilise the piston

Throttle as the throttle is opened, low pressure is created in the vacuum chamber and the piston begins to rise

Needle the piston has a tapered needle attached which blocks the fuel flow. As it is lifted, petrol is drawn up by the low pressure

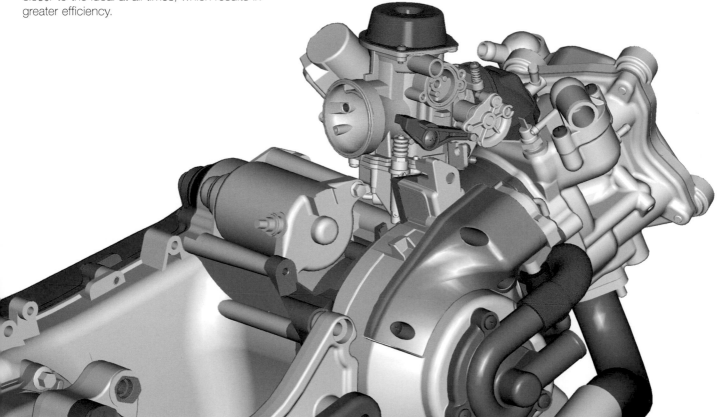

Fuel injection

Fuel injection is not yet found on very many scooters. But it is catching on with most notably many large capacity four-stroke scooters adopting the technology. Two-stroke exceptions include the Aprilia DiTech system described below and the Piaggio Runner Purejet.

A fuel injection system comprises one or more injectors, a number of sensors and a control unit. Unlike carburettors, which are governed by the laws of physics, a fuel injection system has to be told what to do. For this reason, fuel injection systems need a number of sensors.

A cylinder with a displacement of 250cc might be expected to suck in quarter of a litre of air with each induction stroke, but this is not quite the case. Even with the throttle wide open most engines only fill their cylinders between 80–95 per cent full.

Because the engine doesn't always draw in the same amount of air, the sensors tell an ECU (electronic control unit) how fast the engine is revving and how far open the throttle is. Using this information, and being programmed to know roughly how well the engine will fill its cylinder under these conditions, it knows how much fuel to inject.

The amount of fuel flowing depends on three things: the flow rate of the injector, the length of time it's open and the flow rate from the pump. The injector's rating remains the same but the open time and pressure both vary, and these need to be taken into account too.

If the engine is being started from cold, it needs a rich mixture, so the ECU needs to check the engine temperature. The system also needs to know the air pressure – higher pressure means denser air, which requires more fuel to achieve the correct ratio. The ECU determines how long it needs to open an injector to deliver the required fuel. It then sends a timed signal to the injector, which opens and closes a small nozzle in its end. The opening time is milliseconds.

As well as working out the correct amount of fuel, the ECU must also deliver that amount.

The ECU takes huge amounts of information on board; the more it gets, the better the end decision will be.

This is where injectors are better than carbs. By forcing fuel through a nozzle under pressure, it is equally atomised in all conditions. And the smaller the fuel droplets are, the better they can mix with the air. The end result is greater efficiency and power.

Electronics also deliver a greater degree of control to fuelling. Injection allows manufacturers to dictate all aspects of fuelling, which means scooters will become ever more efficient and economical transport as systems evolve.

Aprilia DiTech

We know that two-stroke engines are incredibly efficient for their weight, which is why they have found favour in scooters. But they are difficult to

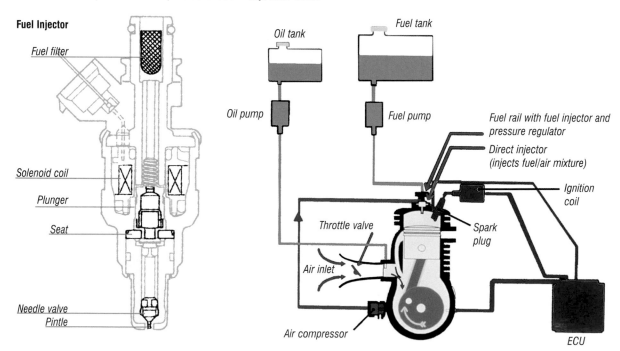

Inside an injector. The actual engineering looks simple, but injection requires complex electronics to control it effectively

Aprilia's DiTech system

Aprilia SR50 with DiTech puts the little scoot at the technological cutting edge

design to burn cleanly, and modern emissions regulations are ruling them out of contention. However, Aprilia's Direct Injection Technology (DiTech) could be the future.

Fuel is injected directly into the combustion chamber, unmixed with two-stroke oil. In a traditional two-cycle engine, the combustion chamber is scavenged with a fuel/air mixture. A considerable quantity of unburnt fuel and oil 'short circuits' the combustion chamber to the exhaust and is discharged. In the Aprilia DiTech system, the chamber is scavenged with air only. The fuel is separately mixed with compressed air and injected directly into the chamber only when the exhaust ports are closed. The oil is delivered by a separate pump, the amounts dictated by the ECU. These elements combine to guarantee the fuel/air mix can't escape.

With the DiTech system, ignition of the mixture is guaranteed with each stroke, thus eliminating the misfire effect of unburnt petrol and oil introduced directly into the exhaust. Perfect combustion is guaranteed because of a stratified charge, where the mixture is rich close to the plug and leaner away from it (down to 30:1 under light loads and 50:1 at idle compared with the 14.7:1 described in the section on carbs).

The highly sophisticated ECU has many sensors. The compressed air is delivered by a cam driven pump at the crank. The fuel pump is small and highly efficient to avoid overloading the scooter's modest electrical generating systems.

Aprilia claims a 40 per cent improvement in fuel consumption, a 60 per cent reduction in two-stroke oil consumption and 80 per cent less exhaust emissions than a conventional two-stroke engine of the same size.

The DiTech engine was fitted to the Aprilia SR50 in 2000, the scooter that established the sports scooter class when it was first launched back in 1992.

Ignition

Ignition is the mechanics of igniting the air/fuel mixture in the combustion chamber. This is more difficult than it first sounds. For starters, the mixture has to be ignited at just the right time to give maximum power. In engines this is measured in degrees of crank rotation before or after the piston is at top dead centre of its stroke.

Four-stroke, four-valve cylinder *A dramatic representation of what happens inside four-stroke cylinders*

In many cases the air/fuel mixture is actually lit before the piston reaches the top of its stroke. The mixture burns, expands and pushes down on the piston – it doesn't explode.

For this reason, the inertia of the crank is enough for it to keep turning despite the burn starting while the piston is coming up the bore. The idea behind starting the burn early is simple – it takes time for the mixture to burn and increase the cylinder pressure.

But time is something an engine is short on (at high revs there are only a few hundredths of a second for the mixture to burn), so by starting the burn early it is more developed as the piston starts on its down-stroke, where maximum pressure is needed.

Also, as the piston travels down the bore, it increases the volume of the cylinder and reduces the pressure, which reduces the effect of combustion. In fact most of the useful work done by the burnt gas takes place in the early stages of the stroke. Ignition is timed to give maximum efficiency on the power stroke.

The burn is started by the spark plug. By jumping a high voltage across a gap a spark is produced. This excites the molecules adjacent to the spark enough for combustion to start. From there, the flame spreads out through the mixture until all the mixture is burnt, or something causes it to stop.

There are several things that can stop the burn. For example, if the mixture is uneven and there are excessively lean areas in the mixture. There will also be small areas around the cylinder wall that don't burn properly because the heat energy that would excite the molecules is absorbed by the metal.

Compression ratios also play a role and are often increased when an engine is tuned. By compressing the mixture more, air and fuel molecules are crammed closer together, which makes it easier for each molecule to ignite the next.

So the conditions have to be right for the mixture to burn. But, if the ignition system doesn't deliver enough voltage, or there's a bad connection, the spark may not be strong enough to ignite the mixture properly or even jump the gap at all. If that happens there will be only a partial or zero burn – a misfire. For this reason it's important to keep the ignition system in good order.

It's also more difficult for the ignition to ignite a lean mixture or one under high compression. In both cases a strong spark is required.

Early and basic conventional scooter ignition systems have flywheel generators to provide the electrical needs, including ignition. The beauty of these was that they don't require a battery to start the engine or power the lights or ignition system. When a wire coil passes through a magnetic field, or indeed a magnetic field passes around wire coils, an alternating current is induced. The flywheel generator feeds power to an ignition source coil via closed mechanical contact breakers to another ignition coil that has a primary winding (with a few turns of wire) and a secondary coil (with many turns). This is called the high tension or HT coil. A cam in the flywheel opens the contact breaker at the optimum time for best combustion, interrupting the flow through the primary winding, which induces a very high voltage in the secondary coil thus causing a spark to jump the plug's electrodes. We have ignition. The best thing about these systems is that they are cheap to manufacture and repair. But they are not maintenance free in that the points gap, condition, lubrication and timing must be checked periodically. They are also only really suited to low-speed engines because the spark cannot automatically advance and retard as engine speeds rise and fall to optimise performance. That's fine on small two-strokes, such as basic scooters, but less desirable on four-strokes and larger engines. They tended to use mechanical automatic timing units to move the position of the cam relative to the crank position so that the contacts open earlier or later in the cycle.

Then along came fully electronic ignitions. These did away with the mechanical contact breaker and allowed the timing to be advanced and retarded electronically depending on engine load. A trigger magnet on the flywheel or rotor causes a pulse to be generated each time it passes a pick-up coil (also known as the pulse generator coil) and gives an electronic means of telling the ignition control box that it's time for a spark.

You're most likely to encounter this system on today's scooters. If there is a downside to modern ignition technology, it is that while many of a system's components can be tested, they can't be repaired and timing can't be adjusted, as it's preset by the factories. So for derestriction and tuning work you'll need to turn to aftermarket suppliers.

One of your scooter's smallest components is also one of the busiest. Meet a spark plug

Exhaust systems,
silencers and catalytic converters

Now that we've seen how scooter engines get their fuel/air mix in and ignited, we need to look at the mechanics of getting the exhaust out. This is about more than the simple expulsion of spent gases. Plainly it's desirable that exhaust gases should be directed behind the bike rather than straight out of the front of the engine into the scooter's bodywork and around the rider. In addition, there needs to be a level of silencing, not just for the rider's sanity, but everyone else's too. Exhaust systems also help to cool the escaping gases, which minimises secondary combustion.

Most exhaust systems are painted steel although some are chrome-plated while others are heavier, but less corrosion-prone stainless steel. At the other end of the spectrum, exotic metals such as titanium are used on sporty race systems.

Part of the exhaust system's function is to assist not only in getting spent gases out, but getting the fresh fuel/air mix into the cylinder.

As we've seen, larger scooters these days are almost exclusively four-strokes. Exhaust systems for four-strokes are designed so that part of the high-pressure wave caused by combustion heading down the exhaust pipe is reflected back up the system. The low-pressure wave that has been following in the wake of the high pressure wave helps to 'suck' the fresh fuel/air charge in through the opening inlet valve while the exhaust valve is still partially open. The component of the high-pressure wave that the exhaust system bounces back prevents the fresh charge from simply heading straight down the exhaust pipe before the exhaust valve can close and compression take place. When the exhaust valve opens again after combustion, the departing high-pressure wave naturally has a low-pressure one in its wake that helps draw the exhaust gas out. Then the whole business starts again.

The whole event is known as the exhaust-pulse-scavenge effect. The design of the exhaust system is critical because the pulses have to occur at the optimum times to make the most of the engine's available power, and to help make that power available at the most useful points in the engine's rev range.

Exhaust design is even more critical for the two-stroke engines we see on the majority of smaller scooters. So much more so that even on twin-cylindered two-strokes (admittedly a rare sight these days) each cylinder will have its own separate exhaust system, while on a multi-cylindered four-stroke the exhaust pipes can be conjoined and exit through a common silencer. As we saw in the section on engine types, two-strokes have transfer ports rather than valves. Crankcase compression plays a key role in compressing the incoming mixture and getting it through the inlet ports and into the combustion chamber, and helps push out the exhaust gases in the process.

On two-stroke systems the exhaust pipe flares out – the expansion chamber – then tapers down to a reverse cone. The gases expand and slow in the widely flared area of the expansion chamber before being slowed suddenly and reflected back by the narrow reverse cone. This creates the high pressure required to prevent the fresh charge escaping unburnt down the pipe before the exhaust port can close fully; it goes so far as to push excess escaping fresh charge back into the combustion chamber. Again the low-pressure wave behind the escaping exhaust gases helps draw the fresh charge in.

Again careful design dictates the points at which this all happens. On a typical scooter sudden surges of power would not be desirable, so they are designed to perform in a reasonably civilised fashion across a wide rev range. A tuned scoot with a race system on the other hand is designed to generate peak power and plenty of it within a narrow rev range.

Mounted to the end of the exhaust is the silencer. Increasingly stringent noise regulations mean that manufacturers have to find ways of keeping the noise down without making them so restrictive that the flow of the exhaust gases is hampered thereby sapping power. A typical silencer has a combination of perforated metal baffles in the pipe part of the silencer with a wrapping of Rockwool-type material held in a can around it. Between them they absorb the worst of the sound waves.

A number of exhaust systems now feature catalytic converters to change the more noxious elements of exhaust gases such as hydrocarbons and carbon monoxide into less harmful water, carbon dioxide and oxygen. A typical catalytic converter is a honeycomb filter containing such catalysts as platinum, palladium and rhodium fitted between the exhaust and the silencer. A catalytic converter is very sensitive to the amount of fuel in the combustion system and its type, which is why they work best on fuel-injected engines running on unleaded petrol.

Two-stroke expansion chamber exhaust system
Spent gases rush out as a high-pressure wave, gradually expanding and losing velocity until reaching the reversed cone. Gases are compressed by the reverse cone and a proportion returns as a reverse pulse. This creates high pressure at the exhaust port, stopping fresh mixture escaping down the exhaust

Transmission

For many scooter riders, a huge part of the appeal is the 'twist and go' automatic transmission. Unlike motorcyclists who have to juggle gearshift, clutch and throttle, the scooter rider just opens up the twistgrip and scoots off into the distance. Scooters with manual gearboxes are something of a rarity now, so we'll concentrate on how the automatic transmissions found on typical modern scooters work.

Most popular of all is the variable ratio belt drive that changes the gear ratio dependent on engine load and road speed. Note that it doesn't change 'gear' as such, simply the ratio between the drive and the driven pulley. The drive pulley is attached to an output shaft from the engine's crank. The drive pulley is connected by belt to the driven pulley on the gearbox input shaft. Connected to the drive pulley, and concentric with it, is a centrifugal clutch. The gearbox input shaft drives a single-speed 'gearbox', which drives the rear wheel.

Open the throttle and, as the engine speed rises, centrifugal force causes the clutch to engage drive. The drive pulley at the front and driven pulley at the rear are each made up of two halves, one fixed and the other free to slide towards and away from the other. The drive pulley's movement is controlled by rollers that ride up and down ramps. As engine speed increases centrifugal force throws the rollers up their ramps, which causes the pulley halves to move towards each other. This has the effect of making the belt ride further from the centre of the pulley's shaft. At the same time the driven pulley, made up of sprung halves, moves apart, because its springs are weaker than the forces pushing the drive pulley together and pulling the belt out on its diameter. The belt is drawn closer to the centre of the separating driven pulley halves. The result is

that the belt is turning on an increasing diameter at the front and a decreasing one at the rear as the engine speed rises. The effect increases as the engine speed rises until the highest 'gear' is attained. Close the throttle (or start climbing a hill) and the engine speed drops, the rollers in the drive pulley start to return down their ramps and the pulley halves move apart while the driven pulley halves correspondingly move back together. The belt goes closer to the centre of the drive shaft and moves out on the diameter of the driven one. The 'gear' is effectively lowered, which allows it to accelerate more effectively as the throttle is reopened, or the scooter slows as the throttle is closed. When slowing to a standstill, eventually there is insufficient centrifugal force and the clutch disengages. Open the throttle and the whole process starts again.

A more sophisticated approach is to dispense with the variable pulleys and use centrifugal clutches to change ratio under varying engine speeds and loads. As the centrifugal forces vary, drive is taken care of by the appropriate clutch.

Some manufacturers are now dabbling with semi-automatic systems as we saw in the chapter outlining the various scooter types. These allow the rider to select between economy and performance modes, holding the ratio they want for cruising or acceleration.

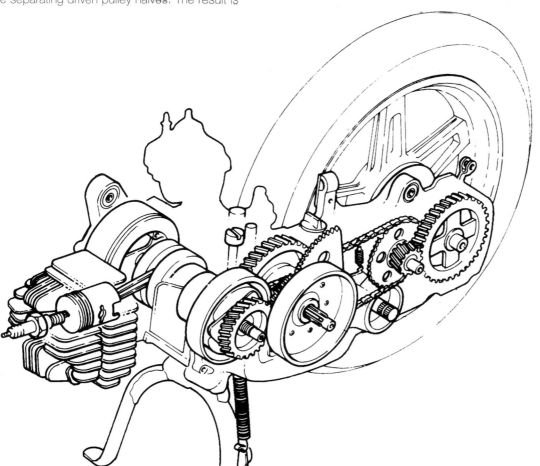

An X-ray view of a typical scooter's simple but clever and effective automatic transmission

Electrics

We've already looked at how scooter ignition systems operate, so in this section we'll concentrate on the other aspects of your scooter's electrics. Apart from the most basic budget machines, many of today's scooters boast a host of electrical niceties that extend beyond the basic lighting systems required to see and be seen.

The majority of scooters currently on the market have 12-volt systems, with power generated by a crankshaft-mounted alternator – so called because it generates alternating current. This has to be converted into direct current to charge the battery and provide power to the lights, and the other electrical devices. A device called a rectifier takes care of the conversion (rectification) of alternating current to direct current and is normally part of a combined regulator/rectifier, because the output level of the alternator has to be controlled (regulated) when too much current is being generated at higher engine speeds. If the output wasn't regulated the system would overcharge and the battery would boil, bulbs blow, and sensitive electrical units would be damaged.

Many scooter owners find electrics daunting, and are put off by their apparent complexity.

Looking at a wiring diagram for even a relatively basic machine, it's easy to understand why so many people are electro-phobes. The schematics often resemble a subway map for some diabolical underworld. But if the elements of the entire electrical system are thought of separately, things become much clearer.

Every scooter requires an ignition system, which we've already looked at. If the scooter has an electric starter, then that forms another circuit. Then there's the charging circuit. Add to those the lighting, indicator and warning light circuits and we have all the fundamentals a scooter requires. Additional circuits might include the engine management system for fuel-injected scooters, accessories such as heated grips and intercoms, and alarms and immobilisers.

For an electrical component to operate it needs a supply of electricity and must be part of a complete circuit. Almost without exception, modern electrical systems are negative earth. Electricity flows from the positive side of the battery, through the component and back to earth – the negative terminal of the battery. If the circuit is incomplete, for example if a wire is disconnected or broken, the electrical component won't work. Many electrical problems where components haven't in fact failed are traced to poor earthing. Instead of connecting all of the components back to a single earth using many long wires, the battery negative terminal is connected to the frame or engine. The electrical components have shorter wires that earth them to the frame or engine to complete their circuits back to the battery's negative terminal.

The battery stores electricity fed to it from the alternator via the regulator/rectifier. It uses this to power the electrical systems when the alternator output is below that required to operate the electrical systems, for example at low engine speeds or to operate an electric starter, where fitted.

Most scooters have an electric start these days, but many still retain a kickstart as backup because many smaller scooters have little batteries that would quickly be exhausted by repeated starts on successive short runs. The starter motor draws a large amount of current, so its power supply lead is made of heavy duty wire – a cable of the lighter gauge used elsewhere on the scooter would melt. To avoid using a heavy duty starter switch, an electromagnetic coil, known as a relay, is used to complete the circuit when the starter switch is pressed. The power goes direct to the motor from the battery, keeping bulky wiring to a minimum and reducing voltage drop across the whole system.

There are two parts to the lighting system. First there are the side and headlights, the tail light, and the lamps that illuminate the instruments. Increasingly countries require that these be permanently on, so many scooters no longer have switches to turn the lights on and off, with the only light switch toggling between main and high beam. Headlamp bulbs are either tungsten filament or halogen. The latter is preferable as they are twice as bright watt for watt as tungsten.

Then there are the direction indicators flashed on and off at the required rate by a flasher relay. A rear brake light is an essential too. Oil level lights for two-strokes and pressure lights for four-strokes feature on most scooters, and there'll be a high beam warning light, indicator 'idiot' lights and occasionally a sidestand warning switch.

Some scooters have a fuel light or gauge, a temperature light or gauge, and there may also be a fuel injection/engine status warning light on injected bikes.

Sensors and switches connected to the warning lights detect the status of the systems they monitor.

Fuses are used to protect electrical components. Some scooters with simple electrical systems have only one fuse, while more sophisticated machines have a number of fuses, individually protecting various parts of the system. The first thing to suspect when electrical problems arise is the related fuse or fuses; these can usually be checked visually once removed.

The last electrical essential every scooter requires is a horn. Not every road user is as switched on or observant as riders of two-wheelers have to be.

Fuses protect key components from electrical overload damage. Sometimes they just fail. Immediate failure on replacement shows there's a more serious fault

Blown

Un-blown

Connectors
A little bit of preventative maintenance will ensure they keep the electricity flowing to where it needs to go

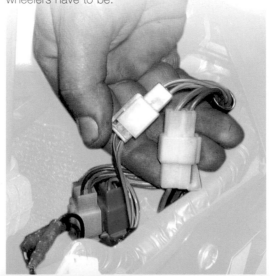

Bulbs do blow now and again, but usually through old age and sometimes vibration. If they persistently fail, there's a problem.

Scooter frames come in a variety of types, but they all have the same basic functions to fulfil. They have to carry the engine and transmission, suspension, electrical systems, all the cycle parts and most importantly the rider.

Frames

Lines are more fluid and the curvature more complex for the 21st century, but the principles that were part of the very first pressed-steel chassis scooters are still in evidence on this modern monocoque

Apart from providing the basis for an attractive and functional machine, the frame also has to keep the wheels in line and the chassis geometry correct under the forces of accelerating, braking and cornering.

As with so many areas of mass-produced machinery, in particular scooters, which were initially intended to provide economical transport, ease of production and cost have long dictated the designs of various manufacturers. In recent years fashion and the need to make models stand out in a busy marketplace, and the emerging breed of maxi/super scooters has seen frame design and philosophy progress faster than they have for decades.

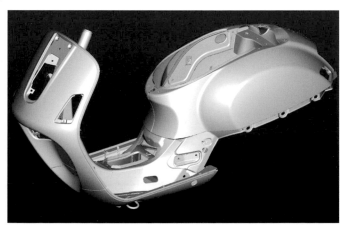

The monocoque

When most people think 'scooter' this is the type of frame they envisage. The pressed steel unit that was both frame and basic bodywork on the first Vespas in the 1940s has been much copied by other manufacturers and lives on in revised and updated form on some Vespa models and their clones today.

Taking the Vespa frame as an example, two large steel pressings form the main part of the chassis. These are welded together along the centre line of the scooter. The legshields and footboards are made from other pressed steel sections that are welded to the main pressings with a tubular steering column passing through and welded to the legshields.

Simplicity itself, and the result is a structure that apart from combining the main frame and the bulk of the bodywork, offers good rigidity for comparatively light weight in a strong package. As this type of monocoque chassis was, and is, easily produced by machine, the amount of labour time required to build the scooter is reduced, which mean the completed item can be sold at a competitive price. This was the main aim of the very first scooters – cheap transport for the masses.

Spine frames

Another take on the simple chassis approach of the monocoque is the spine frame. This is another economical method of frame making. Many scooters have a central spine made up of two main steel pressings, as with the monocoque. Careful design means the frame can accommodate such items as the air filter, battery and even fuel and oil tanks. Lugs, studs and brackets with threaded inserts provide bolt-on points for cycle parts and other ancillaries. If designed to be of square or rectangular section of sufficient size, rigidity is ensured too. The development and more widespread use of plastics and glassfibre for bodywork made this type of chassis increasingly viable because overall weight could be kept down to reasonable levels. An alternative type of spine frame is the tubular type, with a single large diameter tube forming the main central member.

Aluminium beam frames

Drawing heavily on sportsbike practice, Peugeot's Jet Force range and Gilera's DNA are examples of alloy beam frames being used on scooters. This type of frame design offers exceptional rigidity, keeping front and rear ends of the scooter tracking straight and true. Extruded or box-section

aluminium spars are far more resistant to flex than beams made of steel, so an ally frame of equal rigidity to a steel one can be made much lighter. Some might say that the use of alloy beam frames on scooters is solely down to fashion or a desperate attempt to be different. But in fact their popularity will probably increase as discerning riders demand better handling from their scooters, power outputs increase on super scoots, and manufacturers look to incorporate tried and tested motorcycle practice into better built, better handling scooters.

Steel trellis frames

Where the Ducati name is synonymous with the steel trellis frame in the world of motorcycling, Italjet is its equivalent in the world of scootering with its Dragster.

Fabricated from triangular sections made from round-section steel tube, the trellis frame is yet another effective way of attaining the frame Holy Grail – light weight with rigidity. The basic premise of the trellis frame promises good handling, but just to make sure, Italjet has topped off the package with hub-centre steering and a huge alloy wishbone rear 'swingarm' that acts on an adjustable monoshock.

The steel trellis frame combined with lightweight modern bodywork make this type of package viable, but it remains to be seen if other manufacturers will be as blatant in its application as Italjet.

Motorcycle construction principles are beginning to find their way into scooter design and aluminium extrusions are becoming more common, especially on larger machines

Tyres

General

Scooter tyres were once incredibly basic, but the growth in the number of high performance scooters has seen them develop quickly. Nowadays tyres are available that mimic the tread patterns and grip found on sportsbikes.

Tyres have a tough life. The rear transmits the power to the ground, while front and rear have a huge part to play in the handling of your scooter, offering grip in turns as well as in a straight line. Grip is also vital for efficient braking.

Fit the correct tyres for your scooter and the type of riding you do. Don't be tempted to mix and match brands or types, even on a low-performance machine.

Keep tyres at the manufacturer's recommended pressures, which should be checked when they're cold. Under-inflation accelerates wear, ruins handling, raises fuel consumption and lowers the top speed. Over-inflation makes the ride less comfortable and reduces the size of the patch of

tyre in contact with the road; this upsets the handling and causes premature wear. Buy a foot pump and a decent tyre pressure gauge – easier and more accurate than garage forecourt airlines.

Remember to replace the valve caps. At higher speeds centrifugal forces can have the same effect on a valve stem as putting your finger on it. The only thing stopping the air escaping is the valve cap – metal ones with rubber seals inside are best for motorcycle applications.

Wear indicators in the form of little raised ridges across and in the bottom of the tread grooves show when your tyres have reached the end of the manufacturer's recommended safe wear limit. Little arrows or the letters TWI (tread wear indicator) at the 'shoulder' or top of the tyre wall indicate the grooves they're in.

Occasionally other damage such as punctures or tears might mean tyres need to be changed before they wear out. Check for punctures and tears or any foreign objects such as glass or nails stuck in the tread before every ride. Another thing that might lead to early replacement, especially if your regular riding doesn't feature many corners, is that the tyres 'square off'. This is when the tyres lose their semi-circular profile at the centre of the tread.

Tyre types

There are three main tyre types: cross-ply, bias-belted and radial. Radial construction is the most modern and it's fast becoming the most popular tyre type. These almost always run without inner tubes.

In a cross-ply the plies make up the carcass, cross the circumference at around 25–35° and are layered criss-crossing each other. A bias-belted tyre has additional plies under the crown (the treaded rubber bit) to prevent centrifugal expansion under load and slow wear.

The plies in a radial tyre run at 90° across the circumference, with what are called crown plies running at more oblique angles to maintain the profile – a bit like the older bias belts do.

Apart from the carcass there are elements common to all tyres. The bead or tringle is made from wire and holds the tyre to the rim. The bead filler is a rubber insert that helps strengthen the sidewall, which is the area between the bead and the crown (the treaded rubber section). The shoulder is where the sidewall meets the crown.

Buying, choosing and fitting

Rear tyres usually wear out before fronts because the power goes through them. Don't be tempted to mix and match tyre types or use one from a different manufacturer. They are designed and tested in pairs. If your tyres are tubed, fit a new

inner tube too when replacing them. Some radials can be fitted with tubes, but check with the manufacturer's recommendations.

The Haynes workshop manual for your scooter gives instructions on changing tyres, but if you don't feel up to the job, or your tyres are tubeless and you don't have access to a compressed airline, you might want to entrust the job to a tyre fitter. Tyres are directional and must be fitted the right way round. The direction of rotation is indicated by an arrow on the sidewall.

It's a good idea to have new valves fitted to the rims when having new tubeless tyres fitted, as the rubber bodies can harden and perish.

Some makes of tyres have coloured dots to indicate the lightest part of the tyre and the fitter must position this adjacent to the valve. Tyre mounting lubricant or soapy water is used to clean the bead and help it seal. With the stem core of the valve removed, the tyre is inflated to around 50psi until the bead seats. The core is then refitted and the tyre inflated to operating pressure. Control lines concentric with the bead show if the tyre is evenly seated to the bead. If the tyre is not evenly seated, it is deflated and the process is repeated.

The tyre is then balanced, with stick-on weights placed opposite the point the tyre always stops at until the wheel stops randomly when spun. Unbalanced wheels upset handling and accelerate tyre wear.

Puncture repair with mushroom type plugs is possible on some tubeless tyres depending on the severity of the hole. Puncture repair is not possible where the damage is on the sidewall rather than the tread. Different countries have different regulations, and manufacturers give their own recommendations. For safety reasons these are best adhered to. Don't be tempted to patch punctured tubes – use new ones. Tubed tyre punctures, where fixable, should be repaired by vulcanisation to prevent moisture attacking the carcass.

New tyres should be run-in for the first 100 miles or so. The tread of new tyres is smooth and therefore slippy. Running in removes that top layer.

Some words on wheels

Apart from the odd pressed steel wheel on some traditional scooters, most wheels these days are cast alloy. Light and resilient, they can still sometimes be damaged by potholes or riding over kerbs and the like. A certain amount of run out, where the rim is not quite true, is permissible, but too much can seriously compromise handling. If the damage isn't too severe, a rim can be straightened by a specialist. But any suspect wheel should also be checked for cracks at the spokes and elsewhere as these can be invisible to the naked eye. Again this is a specialist job.

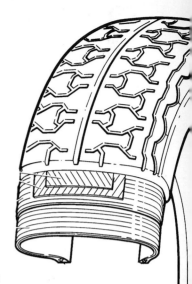

Basic diagram shows typical tyre construction, with crown plies between the tread and inner radial plies

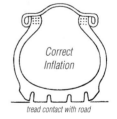

Correct Inflation

tread contact with road

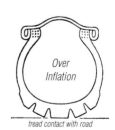

Over Inflation

tread contact with road

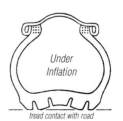

Under Inflation

tread contact with road

Suspension

A scooter's suspension is kept pretty busy. It has to do its best to keep the wheels in contact with the ground over the humps and bumps of road surfaces while at the same time insulating the rider and scooter from the worst that today's roads tend to chuck at us. The importance of keeping the wheels in contact with the road both in a straight line and in corners cannot be underestimated if the ride is to remain stable and the handling adequate.

There are three main types of front suspension found on scooters: telescopic style forks, as found on most motorcycles; leading link suspension; and trailing link suspension.

Telescopic forks comprise a pair of legs, each of which has a tube known as a stanchion that slides up and down inside a casting called the slider, also sometimes referred to as the 'leg'. The wheel spindle is held in the bottom of the sliders. The usual arrangement is to have the stanchion on top and the slider below, known as right way up (RWU) forks. But some machines, particularly sports scooters, mimic the upside down (USD) forks found on many modern sports motorcycles where the legs are above the stanchions and castings on the bottom ends of the stanchions hold the wheel spindle and brake caliper(s). The main perceived advantage of the USD fork is improved rigidity, which, in truth, is not really an issue on a lightweight machine like a scooter. But trick is trick, necessary or not.

Right way up or upside down, the operation of each type is essentially the same. Each leg contains a spring or springs. These take care of the downward motion (dive) of the scooter and the upward movement (rebound). Cheap basic springs, as often found on scooters, have equally wound coils that compress evenly. These are generally adequate for lightweight scooters, but if a particularly violent bump is encountered at speed there is a risk that the forks will bottom out. An improvement is the multi-rate spring system, either two springs of different strengths or a single spring with the coils wound differently at either end. The 'softer' spring, or part of the single spring, absorbs minor bumps and as the going gets tougher, the stronger spring or coils come into play. The next step up is the progressive spring, where the coil spacing reduces along the length of the spring. These become stiffer as they compress and less stiff as they lengthen. The spring strength and coil spacing are calculated to take account of the weight of the scooter, a typical rider, and average riding conditions.

As the suspension goes up and down, energy compresses the springs and is released as they decompress. To prevent the suspension from bouncing uncontrollably and the scooter tying itself in knots, some form of damping is required. Very basic systems rely on friction to do this, but oil passing through valves in the forks takes care of damping on most scooters, controlling both the rebound and the compression of the forks.

A leading link fork has the fork tube finish a short distance behind the wheel spindle centre and a link arm pivoting on the bottom of the fork leg goes forward to the spindle. This link arm is typically connected to the fork by a device similar to a rear shock absorber.

As you might expect a trailing link fork has the link arm pointing backwards.

Leading and trailing link front suspension designs are relatively cheap and easy to make while offering good performance in scooter applications, which is why they still appeal to a number of manufacturers.

Conventional scooter rear suspension sees the engine/transmission pivoting from the frame at the front, while a shock absorber and occasionally shock absorbers, at the other end connect the unit to the frame. Shock absorbers have a damper unit filled with oil, sometimes under gas pressure, inside a spring. This simple arrangement works well on most scooters, where engines are light and performance is modest. The engine/transmission effectively take on a role similar to that of the swingarm on a motorcycle. The weaknesses of this time-honoured design are really only highlighted on higher performance scooters with heavier engines. It's preferable to minimise the amount of weight a two-wheeler carries 'below' its suspension. This is known as unsprung weight. If there's too much of it the momentum it generates sends undesirable forces to the rest of the machine, which means that harder suspension is required. This obviously affects handling and comfort. Shock absorbers can be designed to compensate for and mask some of the problem, but some manufacturers, particularly of certain maxi/super scooters, rather than mounting engines in the traditional fashion, are siting the motors in the main frame. This leaves the final transmission free to pivot on its own more like a motorcycle swingarm without having to carry the full weight of the engine too.

Rear shock showing 'progressive' spring that becomes harder to compress as spring loading increases

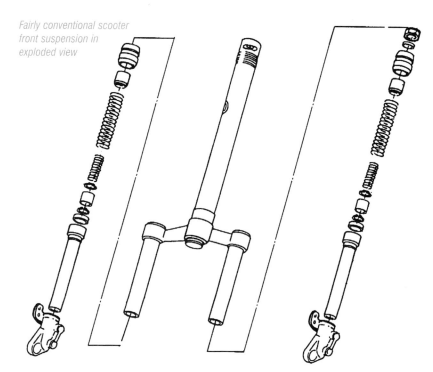

Fairly conventional scooter front suspension in exploded view

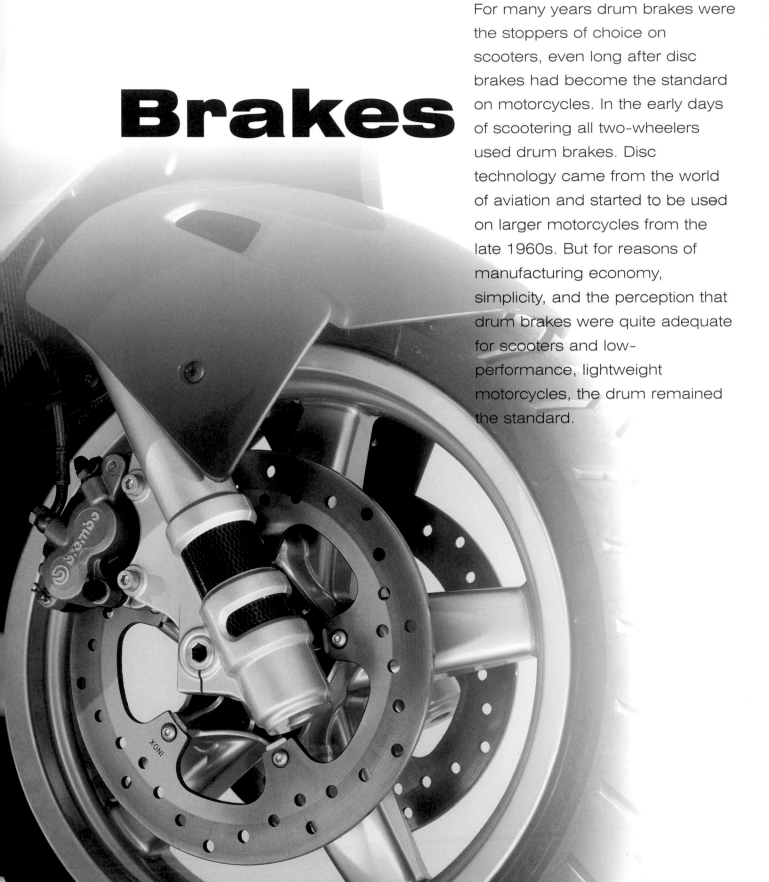

Brakes

For many years drum brakes were the stoppers of choice on scooters, even long after disc brakes had become the standard on motorcycles. In the early days of scootering all two-wheelers used drum brakes. Disc technology came from the world of aviation and started to be used on larger motorcycles from the late 1960s. But for reasons of manufacturing economy, simplicity, and the perception that drum brakes were quite adequate for scooters and low-performance, lightweight motorcycles, the drum remained the standard.

But times are changing, and the drum brake is being used less and less as a front brake, apart from on a handful of budget and smaller scooters. Most sports and larger scooters have a disc, or even twin discs at the front, and rear discs are becoming more common too. Drums are still sometimes used for the rear brake on a few scooters under 125cc, even where there are discs up front. There's no real big deal in this practice, because a two-wheeler needs the majority of its braking force up front as the majority of the weight of bike and rider transfers to the front under braking. So even on an all-disc machine, the rear will be less powerful than the system at the front.

A number of scooters now feature linked braking systems, where actuation of either brake lever partially operates the other brake, balancing the braking forces and relieving the rider of some of the responsibility of applying measured forces of braking to each lever. Anti-lock braking systems are emerging too, similar in principle to those found on cars, where no matter how much braking force is applied by the rider, the wheels can't lock up and cause a skid.

Disc or drum, all braking systems rely on friction to do what they do, converting the kinetic energy of the moving wheel into heat.

Drum brakes

In the case of drum brakes, shoes lined with friction material expand against an iron or steel braking surface integrated into the wheel hub when the brake is applied. The shoes are mounted on a brake plate that remains stationary as the wheel rotates. In a typical arrangement one end of each shoe is mounted on a pivot and there is a cam at the shoes' other ends. Springs are used to hold the shoes away from the braking surface of the wheel until the brake is applied and return the shoes when the brake lever is released. The cam that moves the shoes outwards to make contact with the hub's braking surface has a lever attached to it that is actuated by a cable attached

to the brake lever.

The amount of stopping power generated is dictated by how much leverage is applied through the system. Factors such as the length of the brake lever and how far along it you apply pressure, and the length of the lever at the cam both have a role to play. So does the diameter and breadth of the braking area of the hub, and the area of friction material and its type.

Heat dissipation is important too, if the brake is to retain its efficiency and avoid 'fading', which is where drum brakes lose out when pushed hard, although they aren't worked too hard on scooters in most situations.

Disc brakes

As it's exposed to the elements, a brake disc is far more able to dissipate heat quickly. Operation is usually by a hydraulic fluid system rather than the cable operation of drum brakes. At the lever end is the master cylinder, which contains a narrower piston than the piston(s) at the caliper end (there may be one, two or more moving pistons in the caliper). The difference in the size of the pistons takes advantage of something called the 'hydraulic multiplier effect', which leads to relatively small pressure being applied to the master cylinder by the lever, translating to much greater pressure at the caliper's piston(s). The caliper's piston(s) push steel-backed pads of friction material into contact with the disc, slowing the wheel. The calipers have to be designed so that flex is kept to a minimum to maintain constant pad pressure on the disc, and the diameter of the disc itself is optimised for best leverage to stop the spinning wheel. Piston ratios are carefully calculated so that the brakes are neither too sharp or too soft.

When the brake lever is released the disc pushes the pads away from it and the caliper piston retraction process is assisted by seals in the caliper that twist as the piston moves out so helping to draw it back in as braking pressure is released.

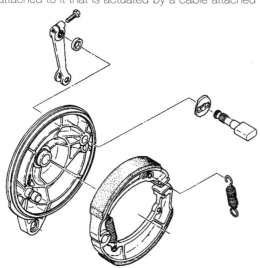

Exploded diagram of typical drum brake still popular on many scooters (left)

Cross-sectional drawing of motorcycle twin disc brakes shows a doubled-up, slightly more sophisticated system than that found on most disc-braked scooters

Bodywork

Well-designed scooter bodywork lends sleek, clean lines to the machine while protecting key components from the elements, dirt and dust. It also partially protects the rider from the wind and rain with legshields and screens. The ultimate protection is afforded by the BMW C1 and Benelli Adiva with their up-and-over roofs.

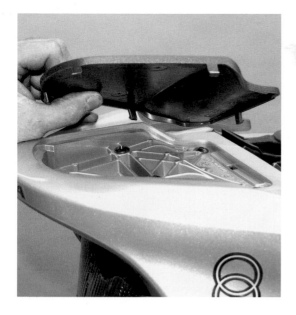

Take care removing ABS plastic panels to avoid breaking tabs (left) and look carefully to make sure you have located every retaining screw (right). There are often one or two hidden just out of sight

Modern plastics have revolutionised scooter bodywork, allowing increasingly complex yet lightweight panels to be created compared to the pressed steel designs of old. Apart from weight savings over steel, plastic panels do not rust. Glassfibre was the first successor to steel and is cheap and easy to mould, paint and repair. The ABS plastics in widespread use today are even lighter than glassfibre and can be more easily formed into extremely involved shapes. It is more difficult to repair than glassfibre although there are some excellent plastic welding kits on the market that can be used by the home mechanic to repair cracks and reattach broken off sections and lugs. More extensive damage tends to mean replacement with a new or second-hand component.

Carbon fibre is the current wonder material for exotic motorcycle bodywork, although it has yet to find widespread use on scooters. It might be light and incredibly strong, but carbon fibre panels are incredibly expensive to manufacture compared to ABS.

The enclosed nature of the typical scooter's mechanicals and electricals mean that some or all of the panels will have to be removed at some point. A scooter's bodywork is reasonably easy to remove to carry out maintenance and repair work on the machine if a few simple rules are kept in mind.

Before removing any panel, check the location and type of fasteners being used. Some of these might be hidden inside underseat compartments and the like, so have a good look around the panel. Fasteners used on scooter bodywork are usually crosshead or Allen head bolts, but trim clips are deployed on some panels, and adjacent bodywork sections may be joined by interlocking tabs that must be carefully separated and joined to avoid damaging the panel's finish. Those tricky-

looking trim clips must have their centres pushed in to remove them. The centres have to be pushed back out before locating them for reassembly. There may also be moulded pegs on the back of some of the panels that locate in and are held by rubber grommets on the frame or brackets attached to it. Sometimes other components like mirrors, seats, battery compartments and passenger footrests have to be removed before a particular panel can be taken off.

Once you're satisfied that you've spotted all the fasteners, you're ready to remove the panel. Take careful note of where each fastener has come from and the position of any washers and spacers to make things easier on reassembly. Put the fasteners in a safe place – it's amazing how easy it is to lose them on a workshop floor or workbench. Should the panel be reluctant to budge, check again for any fasteners you might have missed. Some manufacturers seem to take great delight in hiding the odd fastener in not so obvious locations. Never use excessive force in attempting to remove a panel as it's all too easy to cause expensive damage. When removing larger panels enlist the help of a friend to avoid damaging the bodywork's finish by dropping it on the workshop floor/garden path.

Prior to reassembly check that all fasteners, washers and rubbers are in good condition. Replace any that are suspect. Also make sure that mounting brackets are straight and undamaged.

On replacing panels, take care not to over tighten fasteners. This can place undue stress on panels and cause them to crack. Even if this damage doesn't occur immediately, a panel under stress will eventually crack. Some manufacturers use quick-release type fasteners at stressed points on panels. These turn through 90° to release or reattach, so can't be over tightened.

Tricky-looking trim clips need centres pushed in for removal...

...and pushed back out prior to reassembly

Derestriction and tuning
of 50cc scooters

Most world markets require that 50cc scooters are supplied in restricted form to comply with local licence requirements for young riders. Of course once a rider is of an age and has the right type of licence, there's nothing to stop them derestricting their scooter to enjoy a little more performance.

That's one way of extending the 'shelf-life' of your scooter investment. Most modern scooters have the looks to outpace most sports cars in the car park grand prix, but the reality out on the road is a little different. They might hang tough on the street but simply don't have the power to back up their aggressive looks. Acceleration is not a problem for most small capacity scooters but their lowly top speeds are reached all too quickly. It can get frustrating riding everywhere at 30mph flat out especially when your scooter has been designed with handling and brakes that can easily cope with much higher top speeds.

But all is not lost. Basic derestriction is a relatively straightforward procedure on most models and it's possible to unleash a top speed of between 45 and 50mph without breaking the bank, sometimes without spending any money at all.

Beyond basic derestriction there is a huge pool of aftermarket suppliers and tuning specialists that can supply go-faster goodies and the technical expertise to make the most of your scooter's potential. And that potential can be realised whether your goal is simply to beat your mates round the streets or mix it with the fast folks on the racetrack.

Just remember the basic rule of tuning – there's always a trade-off. Whether that means a less civilised, smooth and tractable ride, poorer fuel economy or compromised reliability depends on how far you take things. For example a race-tuned scooter on urban streets would be a misery, as all the power is usually at the top end and raised gearing will tend to compromise acceleration at the expense of the higher speed needed for racetrack work. And once you've spent a few hours razzing a full-house race motor on the street it'll be time to get stuck into the considerable time, not to mention expense, of rebuilding it.

The trick with tuning is to have all of the elements working together to deliver the type of usable performance you want. The good news is that there's enough headroom even on standard scoots to raise performance safely and reliably.

The scooter

The machine shown below is an aging 1993 Yamaha B Whizz, but nonetheless provides a good example of what can be done. This is the scoot that was at the vanguard of the current sports scooter craze, and was first introduced over ten years ago. Although it's now looking a bit dated, it's still a current model in some countries, and the engine and transmission are still in use on loads of scooters worldwide, so it's a good example to use to show what's available to pep it, and countless scooters like it, up.

Gee whiz it's a tuned-up B Whizz, with considerably more bang for your scootering buck

What does what

Any tuning modification you make to your
scooter's engine has an effect on the
transmission. So let's remind ourselves of how the
transmission works to fully understand what
happens as we go in pursuit of speed.
There are four basic elements.

1 The front pulley

The front pulley is two separate plates forming a
'V' in which the drive belt sits. At low revs the
pulleys are wide apart so the belt sits further down
in the V – this gives a low starting gear so the bike
can pull away. As the revs rise, centrifugal force
pushes the halves of the V together, forcing the
belt to the outside and giving a higher gear for
better top speed.

2 The rear pulley

This behaves in exactly the same way as the front
pulley, but in reverse – low revs mean the halves
of the V are kept together for low
gearing/acceleration, and higher revs force them
apart for higher gearing/top speed. Because the
two pulleys behave oppositely, the belt is
automatically kept at the proper tension.

*Transmission work is
essential in most tuning
efforts. Note trick adjustable
shock absorber poking its
nose in*

3 The variator

This works in tandem with the front pulley. The pulleys control the range of gearing, but the variator controls the RATE at which the gearing changes. It does this with weights that are thrown outwards by centrifugal force up ramps in the variator, in the process forcing the two pulleys together. The heavier the weights, the quicker the gearing rises, the lighter the weights, the longer the gearing takes to raise itself. So if you have an engine with lots of midrange, you can raise the gearing sooner because it will still drive, so you use heavier weights. If you have a peaky engine, you want to keep the gearing down for longer to allow the engine to get up into its power band, so you use lighter weights. Many manufacturers crudely but effectively restrict the top speed of their machines by having a plate bolted concentrically to the variator which prevents the weights from being thrown fully outwards, hence keeping the gearing low.

4 The clutch

This covers the transition from ticking over and not moving, to actually driving along. A steel drum driven from the rear pulley spins round a set of clutch shoes (like a drum brake's shoes) that are pivoted at one end and sprung at the other. At tickover the centrifugal force isn't strong enough to move the shoes against the springs, but as the revs rise the shoes are thrown outwards against the drum. You can change the springs to vary the point in the rev range at which the clutch engages, or you can change the whole clutch for an adjustable one, which can be varied to deal with different conditions and types of riding.

EXHAUST

This is the most popular modification for three reasons. Firstly, the main restriction for most scoots is in the exhaust. There's often a washer or a pipe welded into the header end that can be extracted with the careful application of a Dremel or similar type of tool to grind away the weld holding in the restrictor.

A step up from simple derestriction of the stock pipe is changing it for an aftermarket performance item. But be aware that some of these are not for road or highway use, so you may fall foul of the law if stopped at the roadside. But fitting the right performance pipe can have a huge effect. They can also look very good and trick and are usually a cinch to fit.

Most pipes don't need changes to the carburettor settings, however check with your nearest tuning shop to be sure. But many do come with different weights for the variator which can be tricky to set up right, so if you're not confident in your mechanical capabilities, get an expert to do it. This is a Ninja Super Scoot pipe, check the web for your local distributor. It's not the cheapest of aftermarket exhausts, but it fits straight on, gives a healthy power increase, and has a nice deep tone – many aftermarket pipes sound like a couple of wasps in a bean tin, so that while you might have been frustrated at your scooter's lack of go, the whole neighbourhood is now irritated by your rasping attempts to screw every last gram of power out of your bike.

VARIATOR

You don't strictly need to change this, as you can just change the rollers in the standard item after removing any restrictor plate as described earlier, but a racing variator gives you a smoother and more accurate change in ratios as the revs rise. Fitting one is not difficult, but you may need a special tool to hold the pulley while you undo the nut. The B Whizz was fitted with an Omega Racing Concept variator, which comes with three sets of weights to fine tune the response to suit your other modifications.

CLUTCH

Depending on the level of tune, your scoot might benefit from different clutch springs or even an adjustable clutch. This allows you to choose exactly where the clutch bites, so if you've got a very peaky, powerful engine, you'll adjust it to come in at higher revs to give the engine a chance to spin up nicely.

DRIVE BELT

Opinion is divided on whether the standard belt's up to the job with a tuned engine. It's best not to take any chances in this department to avoid being stranded at the roadside if the standard belt lets go. And there's a possibility of a more frequent irritation in the form of a constantly slipping belt under the new improved load generated by your derestricted/tuned scoot. There is a variety of belts available made from super strong and durable Kevlar. The one above is by tuning parts specialist Malossi.

REAR SHOCK

The B Whizz is not alone in having a very basic rear shock absorber. The rear suspension unit is often one of the first victims when manufacturers are looking to build scooters down a price. This Top Performance shock is anything but basic – it has an anodised aluminium body and adjustable spring preload and damping. This type of shock can be adjusted to suit the type of riding you do, whether it's hard solo blasts or two-up riding with a passenger, or even carrying luggage on a camping trip.

CARBURETTOR

The standard carburettor is often tuned for the scoot's restricted status, so substituting it with a larger bore item can help to boost the power. The only problem is that sometimes they can be hard to set up. This Gurtner Racing carburettor is bigger than standard but fits onto the standard stubs and takes the standard airbox. You also use the existing throttle and choke cables and all the settings are already tuned to your bike's engine so you don't have to mess about with jets. It makes a huge difference to the engine's pick-up.

TYRES

Your tyres are the only part of your scooter in contact with the road, so it makes sense to get the best you can. The B Whiz takes big fat tyres and we wanted a chunky tread pattern, so we fitted some Continental Zippy 2 tyres. Not only do they look the part and grip like leeches, they're pretty cheap too. As we saw in the section on tyres, manufacturers are beginning to take more notice of the needs of scooter riders and are basing a number of their products on the high performance tyres they make for the demanding sportsbike market.

AIRBOX AND FILTER

Lots of performance air filters are available, but you'll need to re-jet the carburettor if you're not sticking with the standard airbox. The airbox is another area where some manufacturers introduce restrictions, this time on the amount of air entering the engine. Plastic snorkels and baffles are the usual signs, and to derestrict their removal will be required. Research the specifics of your particular scooter before committing to butchery. Of course if the airbox is flowing more air the engine will need a correspondingly larger amount of fuel, and this will mean rejetting or replacing the carb with a larger item to compensate.

BIG BORE KITS

If 50cc really isn't enough for you, then there is a variety of larger piston and bore kits available. Most will take a 50 out to 70cc and provide a fair bit of extra go. But they need to be fitted in conjunction with a different exhaust and variator rollers to get the full effect, and may need some carburettor modifications and most likely replacement with a larger unit, so it's best to get this done by an expert. You may also find it necessary to change the final gearing to make the most of the boosted power.

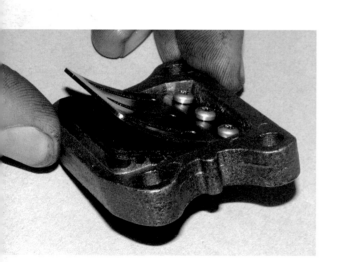

REED VALVES

A two-stroke's reed valves control the induction of the fuel/air mixture and reside just inboard of the carbs. Again stock items can be restrictive while performance alternatives are designed to flow the air/fuel mix easier and more consistently. High-tech materials such as carbon-fibre are found in some performance reed valves.

OTHER FORMS OF RESTRICTION

With the growing sophistication of scooter electronics, manufacturers are finding it easier to restrict performance via the black boxes that control ignition timing, imposing a rev limit to keep performance down. The bad news is that these boxes tend to be 'potted' so that they can't be interfered with by the amateur mechanic, but the good news is that the aftermarket can supply 'plug and play' alternatives that slot straight in to shift the rev ceiling and change the ignition timing.

THE RESULTS

A tuned scooter should be transformed, and only for good reasons, if you've done it right. The long wait for anything to happen when you pull away will be gone, as will the asthmatic, muted exhaust note. In its place will be a deep but still sociable bark from a well-chosen exhaust system and the revs zip up to something useful before the clutch cuts in. Your 50cc scooter will pick up so much speed that you'll find it hard to believe you're on the same machine with its new 50mph plus top speed.

It'll certainly keep up with most traffic though. There's no need to break the bank to get a vast increase in performance. An exhaust fix or swap on its own will give you a noticeable power gain, the carburettor will hike it up again and you only really need the clutch and variator to get into real fine tuning. You can transform a docile 50 into a really practical traffic muncher and almost double its top end speed easily.

THE LAST WORD

No one who's ridden a sorted scooter after riding a restricted one would disagree that the faster one is much, much safer in modern traffic – for one you've got enough power to accelerate out of trouble if you need to. And since the rest of the scoot was designed to go faster anyway, there's usually no need to uprate the brakes and handling. BUT, as soon as you de-restrict your scoot you could fall foul of your riding licence restrictions and the requirements of your insurance policy. It is your responsibility to bear all this in mind before embarking on scooter tuning. Tell insurers what you have done, or plan to do. The premium hike may not be as severe as you expect.

Looking after your scooter

Tools & maintenance	**104**
Cleaning	**108**
Daily pre-ride checks	**110**
Routine maintenance	**114**
Brakes	**126**
Cables	**130**
Bearings	**132**
Electrical	**134**
MoTs	**136**
Storage	**140**
Troubleshooting	**142**
Glossary	**152**
Index	**156**

Tools &
Maintenance

Prevention is always better than cure, as they say. Sticking to a sensible maintenance schedule for your scooter will nip problems in the bud and ensure your scooter is the reliable, convenient transport you expect it to be. As well as helping to avoid unnecessary, costly repairs, timely maintenance will keep your scooter in safe working order.

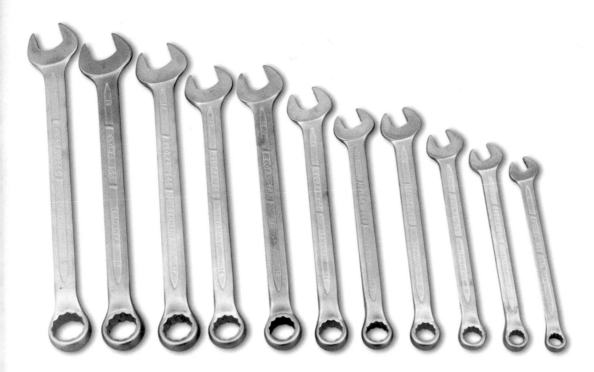

A scooter is basically a collection of components that go round and round, and up and down, so wear and tear is inevitable. In addition, consumables wear out and components work loose.

Your owner's handbook and workshop manual outline the daily, weekly, monthly and annual checks and maintenance tasks your scooter requires. But if you have neither of these books, this chapter explains the basic essentials.

Tools are essential for looking after your scooter properly. Good quality products of the correct type will help you make a good job of things. You don't need to kit your garage or shed out like a main dealer workshop, but having a few quality essentials helps.

Spanners

A set of spanners ranging from 7–19mm is good enough to tackle the majority of the fasteners on most scooters, although you may want to buy two 10, 12 and 13mm spanners as they're popular sizes and sometimes it takes two to undo a component.

Buy combination spanners – they have an open end and a ring end. There are numerous jaw-and-ring designs. The more expensive types drive on the flats of the fasteners rather than the corners. But don't worry too much about this: quality and comfort are the priorities. Buy the best you can afford and, if you find over time that the most commonly used spanners are wearing badly, replace them with higher quality items. Car boot and yard sales are a great source of second-hand tools for people on a budget. Your money might be better spent at one of these rather than on cheap and nasty new stuff.

A couple of small adjustable spanners are also a worthy addition to your toolkit, but they're not as good as non-adjustable types because they are more prone to slipping on fasteners, which causes them to round off.

This ring spanner drives on the flats of nuts and bolt heads, reducing the risk of rounding off through better contact with the component

This spanner offers more angles of attack, but drives on the corners, giving nuts and bolts a harder time

Socket sets

A socket set is vital. As with spanners, cheap stuff is a no-no.

For scooter work, ¼, ⅜ and ½in are the most popular drive sizes, with sockets ranging from 6mm to 24mm in the best sets for scooter maintenance. Most sockets have a 12-point design, which allows the socket to fit in more positions and grip bolt heads and nuts snugly to avoid rounding. However, as with spanners, a six-point design is better in some ways as it is more tolerant of fasteners that have already been slightly rounded. When you remove rounded fasteners it's a good idea to replace them with new ones – you might not be so lucky getting them off the next time.

Allen, Torx and spline bits are available to fit socket drives. Torx and spline-headed bolts are rare on scooters, but where they are used you'll need the appropriate sockets.

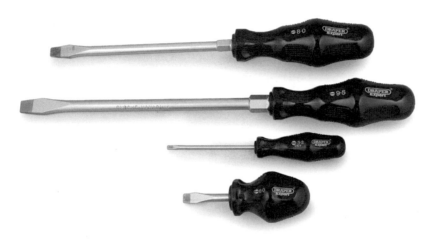

Screwdrivers

It's worth buying good quality screwdrivers as screw heads are frequent casualties of home servicing. This is not always the fault of the home mechanic; the metals used are often of inferior quality. Buy screwdrivers with good tips and comfortable handles. A selection of Phillips, plain cross-head and flat-bladed screwdrivers is enough for most jobs. Be sure to use the screwdriver that best fits the screw slots you're working on. If you intend to strip your engine, an impact driver that can take sockets as well as screwdriver bits is handy.

Allen keys

A good set of Allen keys is essential. The classic 'L' shape are fine, but consider getting a set of T-bars and some socket Allen keys. Use the socket keys to loosen tight bolts followed by the T-bars to spin them out quickly. The most common sizes are 4–8mm, but try to get a few in sizes a little either side of this range. You'll rarely need to use Torx and spline keys on your scooter, but you won't get these types of fasteners undone without a set.

Pliers

As well as a standard set of pliers, long-handled snipe-nose pliers are extremely useful for working on scooters. They allow you to reach deep into the machine through limited gaps. A pair of vice-grip pliers will also make life easier. It's also worth investing in a pair of circlip pliers – you won't need them often, but you'll be glad to have them when you do.

Torque wrenches

When it comes to reassembling your scooter, a torque wrench is handy to ensure fasteners are tightened to the correct figures, as listed in your workshop manual. This will avoid snapped fasteners, stripped threads and distorted casings or worse. There are two types of torque wrench: the beam type, which uses a pointer on a calibrated scale to show the correct figures; and the pre-set type where the torque is set with an adjuster and the tool 'gives' or clicks when the fastener is at the correct tightness. You'll need a torque wrench suitable for scooter work (the majority of settings for scooters are lower than for cars). A range of 7–100Nm should suffice.

Tool care

Look after your tools and they'll give you years of service. A squirt of WD40 and a wipe with a rag after use is wise. Store them in a decent toolbox kept in a dry place. If you try to apply some logic to what tool goes where in the box, you'll save yourself hours of frustration hunting for the right tool.

Other stuff

Some jobs on your scooter will require specialist tools designed by the manufacturer. Because you will require these only rarely, it's best to hire them when necessary. Some owners' clubs also operate tool loan schemes. Invest in a battery charger and a trickle charger for those occasions when the scooter is stored for an extended period of time.

A drain can or tray for oil and coolant is useful. As are an oil can and a grease gun.

A multimeter and a continuity tester will help to isolate electrical faults. Buy a strobe to check timing provided your scooter has provision for dynamic timing. Most do these days.

Other items that will prove useful are a soft-faced mallet, a feeler gauge, bearing pullers and a brake bleed kit suitable for one-man operation.

Cleaning

Cleaning scooters is as easy as it is important. It's easy because the extensive panels that encase most of a scooter make cleaning a cinch. And important because apart from keeping your scoot looking tidy and new for longer, which increases the amount of money you're likely to get when you sell or trade up to a newer model, it's also an ideal way to spot minor problems before they become major headaches.

A range of specialist two-wheeler cleaning potions and implements. Beats a sponge and a bucket full of warm water and washing-up liquid. Although that's better than nothing

The world of motorcycle racing provides all the reasons why you should make yourself a friend of the sponge and bucket. When race bikes are cleaned the mechanics aren't just trying to keep the sponsors happy. As they clean the wheels, they'll be looking for cracks or dents. It's the same with the rest of the chassis and other parts. Cleaning is the best way to discover problems before they get serious.

The first thing is to clean off the worst of the muck, which normally comes in the form of road filth and built up brake dust on rims. A specialist bike or car detergent will cut through the worst of the road muck; residual brake pad dust on rims can be attacked with proprietary brake cleaner, agitated by a small nylon brush (or an old toothbrush will do, just don't put it back in the bathroom rack afterwards). Remember to clean dust from inside the caliper too, and use only brake cleaner or fresh brake fluid. Other solvents might attack the hydraulic seals. Rinse off detergents promptly to avoid any detrimental effect to finishes on bodywork and wheel rims.

Avoid using petrol as a degreaser on any areas where oil build up might be a problem. Apart from being highly flammable, you don't want to get it on your skin; it can also attack some plastic and rubber parts. Applying degreaser by rag reduces the chances of it getting where it shouldn't, for example in the wheel bearings. Use a proper degreaser and look carefully for the source of any lubricant leaks such as two-stroke oil pipe unions and fork seals. A clean followed by a short run can often reveal the source of any problems.

A scooter can be washed with water and household detergent, but dedicated detergent is better than household washing-up liquid.

Top the job off with a thorough polish. There's a bewildering array of specialist cleaning products on the market and silicon products claim to provide longer resistance to dirt build-up. As a word of advice, don't go too mad too often with paint-restoring polishes as these are usually mildly abrasive and you might wind up going through the paint. Use specialist polishes on bare aluminium and chrome if your scooter has these materials.

For general cleaning you can do all these jobs with a common or garden domestic silicon polish – the same stuff you use for dusting the shelves indoors. It's surprising what these polishes will remove from the dirty surface of a well-used scooter. As they clean and polish at the same time you only have to do the job once, but don't let the sprayed on polish dry out in warm conditions as it can be a nightmare to remove.

The golden rule of cleaning is to use a clean, grit-free rag on your screen and paintwork. Screens and panels may need replacing or repainting if deeply scratched by sponges or rags that have been used to wash off gritty road deposits from wheels and chassis.

If you're serious about cleaning, or your scooter gets particularly filthy, you might want to invest in a jet washer. But don't be too vigorous around wheels, head, swingarm and shock bearings, because their grease can be blasted out in the process, which will accelerate wear.

Daily pre-ride
checks

When you use your scooter on a regular basis, it's all too easy to get complacent about making the daily and regular checks that ensure your scooter is safe to ride. But a few pre-ride checks make good sense, regardless of how often you ride, and make it easier to spot problems and wear and tear early. Your owner's handbook lists most of the pre-ride checks you should undertake, but if you don't have a manual, or it's not as comprehensive as it should be, the next few pages cover the key areas to inspect.

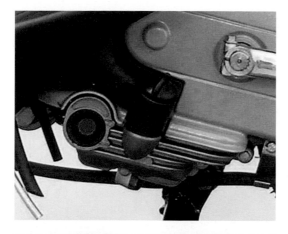

Oil level sightglass and filler on a typical four-stroke scooter engine. Ensure the scooter is off of its stand, upright and on flat ground to get an accurate level reading

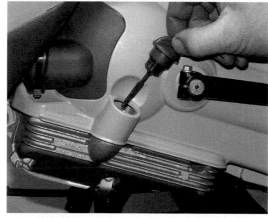

Some machines use a dipstick to check oil level. Depending on manufacturer, the reading should either be taken with the unscrewed dipstick resting on the filler neck, or after it has been screwed fully home

Wipe the dipstick before checking the oil level to ensure that any residual oil on the dipstick does not lead or contribute to a false reading. Again the machine should be upright on level ground

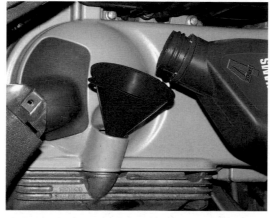

Use a funnel when refilling the sump or topping up the oil. Filler necks never seem to be at the correct angle to pour oil in without some of it slopping down the side of the engine

Engine oil: four-strokes

First put your scooter on its centrestand on level ground. If your machine doesn't have one, get a friend to hold the scooter upright for you.

To get an accurate measure of the oil level, check it when the engine is cold. Otherwise wait for at least five minutes after the engine has been run to give it a chance to cool down. Make sure you have a supply of the correct oil available if a top up is required and be careful not to overfill.

If you find that you often have to add oil, check for leaks. If there is no sign of oil leakage around the engine, it could be burning oil because of worn piston rings, failed valve stem seals or worn valves and guides.

Some engines have a sightglass in the left-hand side of the crankcase. Wipe the window clean if necessary. The oil level should lie between the MAX and MIN level lines.

If the level is below the MIN line, unscrew the oil filler cap and top up with the recommended grade and type of oil, until the level is up to the MAX line on the sightglass.

Other engines have a dipstick on the oil filler cap. Unscrew the cap and wipe the dipstick on some clean rag, then insert the clean dipstick back into the engine and screw the cap fully in. Some dipsticks have to be rested in the filler neck to get the correct reading – check your owner's manual

The oil level should be up to the MAX line on the dipstick. Again, if necessary, top up the engine with the recommended grade and type of oil to bring the level up to the MAX line.

Engine oil: two-strokes

Top-up the oil tank with a good quality two-stroke oil designed for motorcycle oil injection systems. If your scooter is of the old premix type (rare these days) then of course the oil has to be mixed with the fuel. Injector oils are not suitable for this type of petroil system.

On all two-stroke scooters with an oil level warning light, check that the light extinguishes immediately after the engine is started. If the light stays on or comes on while the scooter is being ridden, the oil tank needs a top-up.

But don't rely on the oil warning light alone. Get into the habit of checking the oil when you fill up with fuel.

If the engine is run without oil, even for a short time, engine damage and, soon after, engine seizure will occur. It is advisable to carry a bottle of two-stroke oil in the storage compartment in case such an emergency arises.

So that's where they've hidden the filler cap...

Keep coolant topped up with the recommended mixture. Investigate the cause of excessive coolant loss

If your scooter has a temperature gauge, keep an eye on it. The machine should get up to temperature reasonably quickly and drop off a little when the thermostat cuts in

Handle brake fluid with care. It's very corrosive. Note strategic deployment of rag in this picture to protect plastics and painted surfaces from damage

Fuel check

Take a look in the tank or refer to, but don't completely rely on, the fuel gauge. Use the right type and rating of fuel for your scooter – most run on 95 RON unleaded. Keep an eye out for fuel leaks and repair these immediately.

Liquid-cooling

Coolant must be handled with care because it is poisonous. As with oil, the coolant level should be checked when the engine is cold, with the scooter upright on a level surface. Your owner's manual will tell you where the coolant level is indicated on your scooter.

Keep a supply of coolant available. A mixture of 50% distilled water and 50% corrosion inhibited ethylene glycol anti-freeze is the stuff to use, of the specified type for your scooter. Keep anti-freeze in the system all year round, not just in winter. Do not top up the system using only water, as the coolant will become too diluted to be effective. Tap water is a definite no no.

Do not overfill the coolant reservoir tank. If the coolant is significantly above the maximum level at any time, any surplus should be siphoned or drained off to prevent it being expelled under pressure when the engine's hot.

If coolant is being lost check for leaks and if the problem persists have a dealer pressure-check the system. Also if coolant temperature is consistently very high, the cause must be investigated.

Brake fluid level

Warning: hydraulic brake fluid can harm your eyes and damage painted surfaces, so use extreme caution when handling it, and cover surrounding surfaces with a rag. Do not use fluid that has been standing open for some time, as it absorbs moisture from the air, which can cause a dangerous loss of braking effectiveness.

Support the scooter in an upright position and keep a supply of DOT 4 hydraulic fluid. Wrap a rag around the reservoir to prevent spillage on painted or plastic surfaces if you have to top it up. The reservoir for the brake master cylinders will either be adjacent to the handlebar levers or, where the master cylinders are cable operated, separate reservoirs will be located further down the system.

Fluid in the brake master cylinder reservoirs drops slowly as the brake pads wear, but if the system is using lots of fluid, there may be a leak. Check it out immediately.

Check that the brakes work properly before riding. If the lever is spongy there is probably air in the system and the brakes will have to be bled. Refer to your manual.

Be careful not to overfill with fluid and make sure that the diaphragm and plate under the reservoir cap are correctly situated before tightening the cap.

Tyre checks

Tyres must be run at the pressures listed in your owner's manual or as recommended by the manufacturer for solo and two-up riding. Pressures should be checked when cold, not immediately after riding. Low tyre pressures can allow the tyre to slip on the rim or come off. High tyre pressures lead to abnormal tread wear and unsafe handling. Fuel consumption and comfort can be compromised too.

Always use a quality, accurate pressure gauge.

Check tyres carefully for cuts, tears, embedded nails or other sharp objects and excessive wear. Operation of the scooter with worn tyres is dangerous because traction and handling will be affected.

Remove any stones or nails in the tyre tread, otherwise they'll eventually penetrate through the casing and cause a puncture.

Ensure that the tyre valve body is not perished and that the dust cap and any balancing weights are securely in place. If tyre pressures drop persistently, have them checked and replaced, or repaired if possible as soon as you can.

Tyre tread depth must be above the legal limit. Even if there were no legal requirements, for safety's sake tread depth should be above the limit of the tread wear indicators. Their position in the tread is usually shown by little triangles at the edge of the tread or the letters 'TWI' and an arrow. Don't wait until your tyres are borderline before replacing and check regularly with a tread depth indicator tool or ruler. Directional arrows on the tyre sidewalls show correct tyre fitment for each wheel.

Check tyre pressures regularly with an accurate gauge, and don't rely on those found on footpumps or garage airlines, supposing you can get the latter to fit on your scooter's tyre valves

Keep an eye on your tyres' tread. Not just to look out for wear, but also any foreign objects embedded in the rubber that could lead to punctures

Suspension and steering checks

Check that the front and rear suspension operates smoothly without binding, and that the rear suspension is correctly adjusted and free to travel up and down without fouling the scooter's bodywork or any panniers you may have attached.

Also ensure that the steering moves smoothly from lock to lock.

Look out for corrosion on the front suspension's stanchions, and while you're down there, keep an eye on brake pad material too

Be legal and safe

Lighting and signalling: before setting off, check that the headlight, tail light, brake light, and turn signals all work correctly for your safety, to let others know where you are and what your intentions are as well as lighting your way. A working horn is useful from this point of view too and, like functioning lights, is a legal requirement in most countries.

Safety: check that the throttle rotates smoothly and snaps shut when released in all steering positions. Ensure that the stand return spring holds the stand securely up when retracted. It is also essential that both brakes work correctly when applied and free off when released.

Do the lights work OK? Even if you don't plan to ride at night, the law requires that they function correctly, and many believe that they raise a rider's visibility in the daytime too

Routine
maintenance

Once you get in the habit, regular maintenance becomes a matter of routine. But there are some other jobs that, although they have to be done less frequently, are essential to the reliable running of your scooter. Check your manual for recommended service intervals, expressed in distance or time, and the tasks should be performed whichever comes first. Most routine maintenance can be performed by the home mechanic, but if you have any doubts about your abilities, especially when it comes to components of systems that affect safety, refer to a professional mechanic or your dealer. And remember to be careful around petrol, coolant and other chemicals.

Air & transmission filters

Remove any body panels necessary to access the housing for the air filter, which cleans air entering the carb. Undo any screws securing the air filter cover and remove it. Take out the element, removing any additional screws as necessary. The element will be either paper or foam.

If paper, place the filter face down on a clean surface and tap gently to remove dust and dirt. If you have access to a compressed air line, carefully blow dust and dirt from the element. A damaged or very dirty, clogged element should be replaced.

If the element is foam, remove and wash it in hot soapy water, then blow it dry with a compressed air line or a hairdryer set on the cool setting. Do not wring out the element in case you tear it. If the element is damaged or extremely dirty and can't be cleaned, replace it.

Clean transmission filters in the same way as for air filters.

Most foam filter elements should be oiled before refitting. Use either air filter oil, available in liquid or aerosol form, or make up your own 50/50 mixture of petrol and two-stroke oil. Excess should be squeezed out. Wear suitable gloves and take care not to damage the element by squeezing too hard. Let filters dry for a spell before refitting, ensuring that filter housing seals are in good condition. If they aren't, replace them.

Battery

See the electrical section in this chapter for advice on batteries.

Brakes

See the braking section in this chapter for advice on brakes.

It is almost always necessary to remove a panel or two to access filters

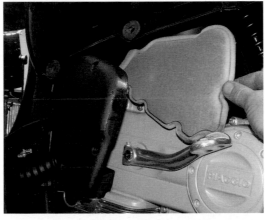

Foam elements can be cleaned and reused provided that soiling is not excessive and the element is undamaged

Paper elements can be cleaned as per the instructions in the text, but excessively clogged units will require replacement

Again this style of foam element can be cleaned and reused provided that it is in good condition

Cooling system

Liquid-cooled scooters should have the entire system regularly inspected. Before undertaking any inspection or work, be sure that the scooter is thoroughly cool. The engine and cooling system can retain heat for a long time after the machine has been run.

Apart from your daily check of coolant level, the entire system should be periodically looked at for leaks. Each coolant hose and pipe should be inspected along its length and at joins and unions, as should the areas around the head gasket, where coolant enters and exits the engine's water jacket, and around the coolant pump. This will mean removing much of the bodywork to provide easy access. Pipes can perish and crack, or become damaged through rubbing against other components. Squeeze the hoses along their length. They should be firm, but flexible, and regain their shape when you stop squeezing them. If they have become hard, they are beginning to perish and should be replaced.

If you find signs of leakages at joins and unions in the system, tighten the hose clips, but not so much that they cause the hose or union to collapse.

Next thing to look at is the radiator, which should be inspected for leaks as well as physical damage. Also make sure that the radiator is carefully cleaned to remove dirt and dead insects from the fins. Otherwise its efficiency will suffer because air can't effectively get to the fins to cool them. Check also for bent or damaged fins. Bent fins can be gently bent back with a screwdriver, but if more than a third of the radiator's area is affected, replace the radiator or have it repaired.

Leaks from a radiator will leave scale deposits or coolant stains below the leak. A leaking radiator can be repaired, but if the damage or corrosion is too expensive, replacement is the only option.

If the cooling system is leaking from any point, don't be tempted to use car-type radiator sealants as they can block the narrower waterways found in scooter coolant systems.

Look at the coolant in the reservoir. If it is discoloured or full of scale, the system should be drained, flushed out and refilled with fresh coolant in accordance with the procedure in your scooter's workshop manual. To test that there's sufficient antifreeze in the coolant, and that there is the right concentration, use an antifreeze hydrometer. If this indicates that the coolant is no longer up to the job, then the system will have to be drained, flushed and refilled.

Always run the scooter, let it get up to operating temperature, then check for any leaks after undertaking any work on your machine's cooling system.

If your coolant level drops inexplicably, and there are no apparent leaks, have the system

Check condition of coolant hoses and ensure that clips are correctly positioned and secured. Look out for leaks, not just around the hoses but at the coolant pump too

Radiators should be free of road dirt and debris that can impair their efficiency. Again look out for leaks and damage to delicate fins

pressure-checked by a dealer.

If the system does need draining, flushing and refilling, first allow the engine to cool completely. Never let antifreeze get in contact with your skin or the painted or plastic surfaces of the scooter. Rinse off spills immediately with plenty of water. Antifreeze is highly toxic, so never leave it lying around in an open container or in puddles on the floor – children and pets are attracted by its sweet smell and may drink it. Check with local authorities (councils) about disposal of antifreeze. Many communities have collection centres that will dispose of antifreeze safely. Antifreeze is flammable too, so store carefully.

To drain, remove the cap from the coolant reservoir. If there is a hissing sound as you unscrew it, there is still pressure in the system, so do not unscrew any further until the hissing stops.

Position a suitable container underneath the lowest detachable point on the lowest coolant hose unclip and detach the coolant hose. Allow the coolant to completely drain from the system.

Now flush the system with clean tap water by inserting a garden hose in the reservoir filler neck. Allow water to run through the system until it flows clear and clean from the detached hose. If there is a large amount of rust or sediment in the water, remove the radiator and flush it out separately.

Reconnect the coolant hose and secure it with its clip then fill the cooling system by pouring clean water mixed with flushing compound into the reservoir filler. Check that the flushing compound is safe for use with aluminium, and adhere to the manufacturer's instructions. Fit the reservoir cap then start the engine and allow it to get up to normal operating temperature. Let it run for about five minutes. Stop the engine, allow to cool then remove the reservoir cap carefully and drain the system again as before. Reconnect the hose, refill with clean water, run the scooter up and drain again.

Now refit the hose and refill the system with the correct coolant mixture, pouring it slowly into the reservoir filler to minimise the amount of air getting into the system. Some systems will have to have the water pump bled after filling; on others it will be necessary to connect a bleed pipe between the pump and the reservoir while filling. Refer to your manual.

Once the coolant is up to the MAX level mark on the reservoir, refit the cap. Now put the scooter on its centrestand so that the rear wheel is clear of the ground. This may mean putting a piece of wood or similar under the stand to raise the wheel sufficiently. Start the engine and let the scooter idle for two to three minutes. Gently rev the engine a few times then switch it off. Allow the engine to cool then remove the reservoir cap. Check that the coolant level is still at the MAX mark. Top up if necessary, then refit the cap.

Check the system for leaks, as described above, and remember to ensure that coolant is properly disposed of. Don't just pour it down the drain.

Two-stroke cylinder head and piston/barrel decoke (decarbonisation)

Modern fuels and two-stroke oils mean it is unnecessary to decarbonise as frequently as in the past. But if your riding involves a lot of short journeys where the engine doesn't get up to full operating temperature for a prolonged period, you will need to decoke at least as often as your service schedule recommends.

First remove the cylinder head as per the instructions in your manual. Remove all accumulated carbon deposits from the cylinder head's combustion chamber using a blunt scraper of hard wood or very soft alloy or copper. The cylinder head and piston are made of relatively soft aluminium, so care must be taken not to gouge or score the surface when scraping. Turn the engine over until the piston is at the very top of its stroke. If the head studs also secure the barrel to the crankcases, hold the barrel down to

Drain coolant carefully and dispose of responsibly. Remember that it is poisonous and can retain a lot of heat even after the scooter has been allowed to cool for a while

avoid disturbing the base gasket. Smear grease around the edge of the piston to trap any particles of carbon, then scrape the piston crown clean, again taking care not to score or gouge it or the cylinder bore.

Clean out the carbon, then lower the piston and carefully wipe away the grease and any remaining particles. Also scrape or wipe clean the intake and exhaust ports in the cylinder. If the exhaust port is heavily coked, the exhaust system will probably also require cleaning as well.

Finish the piston head and combustion chamber off using a metal polish. A shiny score and gouge-free surface is more resistant to the build-up of deposits. Now reinstall the cylinder head in accordance with your manual's instructions.

Drive belt – inspection and renewal

Remove the transmission drive belt cover, then inspect the belt as described in your manual and renew it if necessary. If unusual or fast wear are detected, inspect the pulleys and the rest of the transmission system.

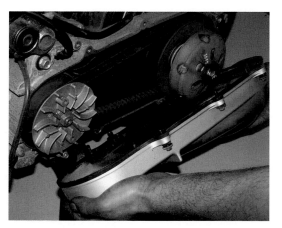

Regular visual checks in between recommended replacement intervals will allow you to ensure that the drive belt is in good condition

Engine oil and filter – four-strokes

Regular routine oil and filter changes are the single most important maintenance procedure you can perform on a four-stroke engine. The oil not only lubricates the internal parts of the engine, but it also acts as a coolant, a cleaner, a sealant, and a protector. Because of these demands, the oil takes a terrific amount of abuse and should be replaced often with new oil of the recommended grade and type. Any savings you make by buying a cheap oil as opposed to a good quality oil will pale into insignificance if your engine gets damaged.

On some engines the oil filter only has to be renewed every other change, for other scooters it is suggested that this is done with every change. Many engines also feature gauze oil strainers that have to be cleaned when the oil is changed. Oil drains best when the engine is warm, but take care when draining the oil, because the exhaust pipe, the engine, and the oil itself can cause severe burns.

Warm the engine so the oil will drain easily, then stop the engine and turn the ignition *off*. Put the scooter on its centrestand on a level surface, and position a clean drain tray below the engine.

Unscrew the oil filler plug to vent the crankcase. This will also help to remind you that there is no oil in the engine. Next unscrew the oil drain plug from the bottom of the engine, and allow the oil to flow into the drain tray. It's best to discard the drain plug's sealing washer and replace with a new one on reassembly, even if it appears to be in good condition.

Remove any oil strainer fitted, as detailed in your manual. Clean the gauze in solvent and remove any debris caught in the mesh. Check the gauze for splits or holes and renew it if necessary. Install the strainer, fit a new sealing washer or O-ring to the plug if necessary, then install the plug and tighten it securely.

When the oil has completely drained, fit the drain plug using a new sealing washer, and tighten it to the torque setting in your manual. Avoid over tightening, or you'll damage the threads.

If due for renewal, place the drain tray below the oil filter. Unscrew the filter or cover over it (note that there is sometimes a spring behind the cover holding the filter in the correct position). Tip any remaining oil into the drain tray. Any O-rings and seals to do with the filter or its housing should be removed. Tighten filter-housing bolts to the torque settings in your manual. Avoid over tightening or you'll damage the threads.

Refill the engine to the proper level using the recommended type and amount of oil. As there is some oil left in the engine during an oil change, you won't need to use the whole amount specified

Remove filler cap/dipstick to facilitate quicker draining of used engine oil. Leave it somewhere prominent to remind you to refill the sump before riding off!

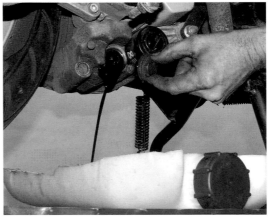

A cut-down oil container or similar makes a useful and cheap reusable drain tray. Oil is best drained when warm, but take care not to scald yourself

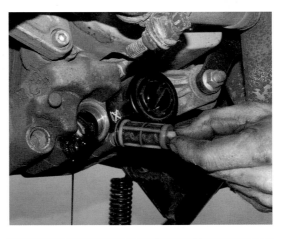

Gauze filters should be removed, inspected and cleaned and refitted provided they are in good condition, if not they must be replaced

Disposable oil filter elements such as these cannot be cleaned out and should be replaced at the recommended intervals. Sometimes at every oil change, otherwise every other oil change

in your scooter's manual and be careful not to overfill. Install the filler plug and tighten it by hand. Start the engine and let it run for two or three minutes. Shut it off, wait five minutes, then check the oil level. If necessary, add more oil to bring the level up to between the level marks on the sightglass or dipstick. Check around the drain plug and the oil filter/strainer areas for leaks.

The old oil drained from the engine cannot be re-used and should be disposed of properly. Check with your local refuse disposal company, disposal facility or environmental agency to see whether they will accept the used oil for recycling. Don't pour used oil into drains or onto the ground.

Check the old oil carefully – if it is very metallic coloured, then the engine is experiencing wear from break-in (new engine) or from insufficient lubrication. If there are flakes or chips of metal in the oil, then something is drastically wrong internally and the engine will have to be disassembled for inspection and repair.

Fuel system

Warning: petrol is extremely flammable, so take extra precautions when you work on any part of the fuel system. Don't smoke or allow open flames or bare light bulbs near the work area, and don't work in a garage where a natural gas-type appliance is present. If you spill any fuel on your skin, rinse it off immediately with soap and water. When you perform any kind of work on the fuel system, wear safety glasses and have a fire extinguisher suitable for a Class B-type fire (flammable liquids) to hand.

To check the fuel system, remove any body panels necessary to gain access to the fuel tank, tap, fuel pump (where fitted) and carburettor. Inspect the tank, tap, pump and the fuel and vacuum hoses for signs of leakage, deterioration or damage; in particular ensure that there is no leakage from the fuel hoses. Replace any hoses that are cracked or perished.

If a fuel tap or pump is leaking they must be renewed as it is rarely possible to rebuild them. If the carburettor gaskets are leaking, the carburettor should be disassembled and rebuilt using new gaskets and seals. While you're in there, clean out the components, and air and fuel drillings with carb cleaner. Do not use pins or any sharp objects in the drillings.

Fuel filters should be cleaned or replaced after high mileages or if contaminated fuel has been inadvertently used. Otherwise fuel starvation will lead to poor performance. Fuel filters can be found in the tap at the union with the carb; sometimes there's an in-line filter in the fuel line. Check gauze filters for tears, dirt and sediment. Fuel tap O-rings will usually have to be replaced if disturbed, and certainly if damaged.

Check around the fuel tap for signs of leaks and ensure that hoses have not perished or gone stiff

Likewise, make similar checks in the area of the fuel pump

Fuel feed to the carburettor should be inspected and the unit itself checked for leaks. In the case of two-strokes, take a look at the oil feed pipe too where applicable

Fuel filters are a useful line of defence to prevent debris getting into the float bowl and narrow drillings of the carb. They must be fitted the right way round and usually have an arrow showing the direction of fuel flow

Check the level of lubricant in the transmission using the dipstick where fitted...

...or the level plug as in the case of this machine. Note that the scooter should be off its stand, upright and on level ground in both cases

Fill to the required level using a pressure oil can filled with the correct grade of lubricant. Go slowly so as not to overfill

Transmission drain and level screws should be correctly tightened and their sealing washers are best replaced every time the screws are disturbed

Transmission oil-level check and change

Have the scooter held off its centrestand on level ground. Some scooters are fitted with an integral filler cap and dipstick and some have an oil level plug. Check your manual. Unscrew the filler cap or plug from the transmission casing. Discard the filler plug sealing washer as a new one should be used on reassembly.

On scooters with a dipstick, use a clean rag or paper towel to wipe off the oil. Check in your owner's manual for how to test the oil level on your specific machine. On some scooters the dipstick has to be fully screwed back into the casing when the level reading is being taken; on others the dipstick must be rested in the filler neck.

Do not risk underfilling or overfilling the gearbox as a transmission seizure or dangerous oil leakage contaminating the rear tyre may result.

On scooters with level plugs, remove the plug – the oil level should come up to the lower threads so that it is just visible on the threads; on others the oil should be just starting to emerge from the level plug hole. Again refer to your manual.

If the oil level is below the appropriate line on the dipstick, or below the level of the plug threads, top the gearbox up with the recommended grade and type of oil. Use a pump-type oil can to top up gearboxes with a level plug. Do not overfill.

Install the filler cap and tighten securely by hand, or fit a new sealing washer to the level plug and tighten it securely.

To change transmission oil, first remove the exhaust system and rear wheel if required to gain access to the drain plug and place a clean drain tray below the gearbox. Unscrew the filler cap or level plug depending on which scooter you have to help the oil drain. Unscrew the oil drain plug, and let the oil flow into the drain tray. Discard the sealing washers on the drain and level plugs because new ones should be used.

When the oil has completely drained, fit the drain plug using a new sealing washer, and tighten it securely. Use a correctly set torque wrench to avoid over tightening and damaging the casing.

Refill the gearbox to the proper level using the recommended type and amount of oil. Install the filler cap and tighten it securely by hand, or fit a new sealing washer to the level plug and tighten it securely.

Check the oil level again after riding for a few minutes and, if necessary, add more oil. Check around the drain plug for leaks.

The old oil drained from the gearbox cannot be re-used and should be disposed of properly. Check with your local refuse disposal company, disposal facility or environmental agency to see whether they will accept the used oil for recycling. Don't pour used oil into drains or onto the ground.

Headlight check and adjustment

A badly adjusted headlight may cause problems for oncoming traffic or provide poor, unsafe illumination of the road ahead. Before adjusting the headlight aim, be sure to consult with local traffic laws and regulations.

Most scooters have adjustable headlights. Refer to your manual for the location of the adjuster screws and the directions they should be turned in to effect up and down movement. Before making any adjustment, check that the tyre pressures are correct and the suspension is properly adjusted. Make any adjustments to the headlight aim with the machine on level ground, with the fuel tank half full and with an assistant sitting on the seat with the scooter off of its stand. If the bike is usually ridden with a passenger on the back, have a second assistant to do this.

Idle (tickover) speed – check and adjustment

The idle speed should be checked and adjusted when it is obviously too high or too low, which will cause the engine to race if too high, or falter and stall if too low. Before adjusting the idle speed, make sure the valve clearances (four-stroke engines only) and spark plug gap are correct. Turn the handlebars from side to side to see if this has any effect on the idle speed. If it does, the throttle cable may be wrongly adjusted or routed, or possibly worn out. This can be dangerous and may lead to a loss of control of the scooter. Refer to the section on cables later in this chapter and rectify the problem before proceeding.

The engine should be at normal operating temperature before adjusting the idle speed. This is usually reached after 10 to 15 minutes of stop-and-go riding. Put the scooter on its centrestand and make sure that the rear wheel is clear of the ground. If your scooter has a rev counter (tachometer) the procedure is easier as you can compare the engine speed your scooter is idling at with that specified in your manual. In the absence of a rev counter, which few scooters have, make sure that at idle (with the twistgrip fully closed) the engine speed is steady and does not falter; it should also not be so high that the automatic transmission engages and the wheel starts to turn.

The idle speed adjuster screw is usually found on the carburettor, or there may be a remote cable and screw nearby. With the engine idling, turn the screw to increase and decrease idle speed.

For your own safety and to meet legal requirements, the headlight must be properly adjusted. You may find that you need to adjust it if you regularly carry a passenger

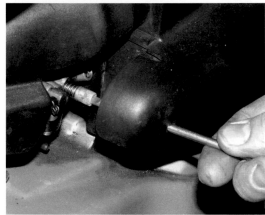

Keep the idle speed right. Not so low that the scooter stalls, but not so high that scooter engages drive the instant the engine is started. Access to the throttle stop screw is easy here…

…less easy on this scooter where the carburettor has to be exposed to get to the adjuster

Snap the throttle briskly open and shut a few times, then recheck the idle speed. If necessary, repeat the adjustment procedure.

If a smooth, steady idle can't be achieved, the fuel/air mixture may be incorrect due to a dirty air filter, blocked carb or fuel lines, or incorrect float height. One other potential cause is that the adjuster cable has run out of adjustment and a replacement is required.

With the idle speed correctly adjusted, recheck the throttle cable freeplay and adjust accordingly (see the cable section in this chapter).

Nuts and bolts – tightness check

Vibration can loosen fasteners, so all nuts, bolts, screws, etc. should be frequently inspected and checked for tightness.

Special attention should be given to the following:
o Spark plug
o Carburettor clamps
o Engine oil drain plug (four-stroke engines)
o Stand bolts
o Engine-mounting bolts
o Suspension and swingarm bolts
o Handlebar lever clamp bolts
o Wheel bolts
o Brake caliper and disc-mounting bolts (disc brakes)
o Brake hose banjo bolts (disc brakes)
o Exhaust system bolts/nuts
o Transmission drain plugs

Equip yourself with a torque wrench and use it to tighten key fasteners to the correct torque settings as specified in your owner's or workshop manual.

Secondary air system – clean

Some scooters with catalytic converters have secondary air systems whose filters and valves must be periodically inspected and cleaned or replaced. Refer to your manual for locations and the correct maintenance procedures.

Spark plug gap: check & adjustment

Some scooters have their spark plug(s) well tucked away, but don't use this as an excuse to avoid maintenance of these crucial components. Ensure that the engine and exhaust system are cool before attempting to remove a spark plug.

Use the correct size spark plug socket – there should be one supplied among the mainly cheap and nasty tools that came with your scooter. You will almost certainly have to remove the engine access panel or side cover from your scooter, and any engine cowl over the cylinder head too.

Pull the spark plug cap off the spark plug, then unscrew the plug from the cylinder head.

Inspect the electrodes for wear. Both the centre and side electrode should have square edges and the side electrode should be of uniform thickness. Look for excessive carbon deposits and evidence of a cracked or chipped insulator around the central electrode. On a correctly running engine the spark plug's insulator nose deposits should be straw brown in colour. White deposits indicate lean running and overheating, while dark or black oily deposits point to rich running or possible engine problems. Check the threads, the washer and the ceramic insulator body for cracks and other damage.

If the electrodes are not excessively worn, and if the deposits can be easily removed with a wire brush, the plug can be re-gapped using a spark plug gapping tool and/or feeler gauge and re-used. If in any doubt as to the condition of the plug, replace it with a new one, as they are not expensive.

Spark plugs can be cleaned by sandblasting, so long as they are cleaned with a high flash-point solvent afterwards.

Before installing a new plug, ensure it is of the correct type for your scooter as per the specifications in your manual. Check the gap between the electrodes. Compare the gap to that specified and adjust as necessary. If the gap must be adjusted, bend the side electrode only and be very careful not to chip or crack the insulator nose. Make sure the washer is in place before installing the plug.

Because cylinder heads are made of aluminium, which is soft and easily damaged, thread the plug into the head by hand. Once the plug is finger-tight, the job can be finished with the plug socket. Take care not to over tighten the plug. You don't want to strip the thread although a stripped plug thread in the cylinder head can be repaired with a thread insert. Now reconnect the spark plug cap and replace any engine cowl and the bodywork.

The spark plug(s) may be well hidden away for protection from the elements, but make plugs a regular part of your maintenance schedule

Speedometer cable and drive gear - lubrication

Some scooters have electronic speedometers, so there's no need for maintenance here. For mechanical speedometers, remove the speedometer cable from the machine. Withdraw the inner cable from the outer cable and lubricate it with motor oil or cable lubricant. Do not lubricate the upper few inches of the cable as the lubricant may travel up into the instrument head. Lubricate the cable in a clean environment to avoid picking up any grit that could grind away inside.

Remove the drive housing and clean all the old grease from the speedometer drive gear/drive housing using degreaser if necessary to get it all out, then lubricate the components with clean grease and reassemble them.

Centre & sidestands

Stand pivots are exposed to road dirt and the elements, so they should be cleaned and lubricated periodically to ensure safe and trouble-free operation.

In order for the lubricant to be applied where it will do the most good, the component should be disassembled. But if chain or cable lubricant is being used, it can be applied to the pivot joint gaps and usually works its way into the areas where friction occurs. If motor oil or light grease is being used, apply it sparingly as it may attract even more dirt, which could cause the pivots to bind or wear more quickly.

The return springs should be able to retract the stands fully and keep them in the retracted position while you're riding. Lazy or broken springs should be replaced. As the springs are very strong, use a spring puller tool as used on motorcycle race exhaust systems. A flapping or sagging stand can dig into the ground when the scooter is on the move, potentially causing an accident.

Steering head bearings

See the section on bearings later in this chapter.

Speedometer drive and cable must be kept clean and lubricated. Ensure correct location of speedo cable inner to the speedometer drive

Pliers may be necessary to get some purchase on the knurled nut that holds the speedo cable to the speedo head

Sidestand springs don't stay this clean for long because road dirt is attracted to the grease or oil that has to be used on pivots and springs. Dismantle and grease regularly

Suspension check

It is vital to the safe control, stability and handling of your scooter that suspension components are maintained in perfect condition. Loose, worn or damaged suspension parts affect a scooter's stability and control as well as compromising rider and passenger comfort.

Front suspension

Stand alongside the scooter and apply the front brake while pushing the handlebars down repeatedly to compress the suspension. You're looking for smooth movement of the suspension without binding and stiction, where the fork seals and bushes prevent the forks from compressing and decompressing smoothly. If this happens the suspension will have to be dismantled and inspected.

If your scooter has a monoshock front end, check the shock for fluid leaks and ensure that its mountings are tight and the bushes are in good condition. Leaky shocks should be replaced, as rebuilding is rarely economical.

On scooters equipped with telescopic forks, check the area around the dust seals for signs of grease or oil leaks, then carefully lever off the dust seal using a flat-bladed screwdriver and inspect the area behind it. If corrosion due to the ingress of water is evident, the seals must be renewed. Refer to your workshop manual for the correct procedure. Exposed chrome plating on fork stanchions can corrode and pit, which can lead to the fork seals being torn and damaged. So keep the stanchions as clean as possible and spray them regularly with a rubber- and plastic-friendly rust inhibitor. If there is any corrosion or pitting apparent, treat them as soon as possible before they deteriorate further. Finally, check that all suspension-related nuts and bolts are tight in case any have worked loose.

Rear suspension

If you scooter is equipped with twin rear shocks, both must be in good condition. If either is faulty, they must be renewed as a pair or the suspension will not work properly and handling will be compromised.

Inspect rear shock(s) for fluid leaks and tightness of mountings. Leaking shocks should be replaced as rebuilding is rarely economical.

With the help of an assistant to steady the scooter, compress the rear suspension several times as you did for the front. The suspension should move up and down freely without binding. If you feel binding, the worn or faulty component must be identified and renewed. The problem could be due to the shock absorber or the pivoting bush or bearing assembly between the engine unit and the frame.

Support the scooter so that the rear wheel is off the ground. Grab the engine at the rear and attempt to rock it from side to side – there should be no discernible freeplay between the engine and

Even with a guard as fitted here to repel road dirt, it still gets on the stanchions and can lead to seal wear. Keep those shiny bits clean

When prising up dust covers to check oil seals, take care not to damage the soft plastic or rubber

A plastic shroud on some shocks between spring and damper prevents dirt getting to the more sensitive moving parts

frame. If there is movement, inspect the tightness of the bush/bearing assembly and engine mounting bolts. Ensure the bolts are correctly torqued as per your manual and check again for movement. If you can still feel movement, disconnect the shock at its lower mounting point and check the swingarm again. Any movement will now be even easier to detect. If there is movement, then the bush/bearing assembly will require closer inspection.

With the shock(s) reconnected, grab the top of the rear wheel and pull it upwards – there should be no discernible freeplay before the shock absorber begins to compress. If there is, the shock absorber mountings are worn and will have to be renewed.

Valve clearances – check and adjustment (four-stroke engines)

The engine must be completely cold for this maintenance procedure otherwise the valve clearances cannot be accurately checked. Let the machine cool for several hours, preferably overnight, before attempting to check and set the clearances.

Remove any body panels necessary to gain access to the alternator (to allow the engine to be turned over with a spanner or socket on the alternator nut) and the cylinder head.

Remove the spark plug to make it easier to turn over the engine and remove the valve cover(s). Discard the cover gaskets or O-rings as new ones should be fitted on reassembly.

Turn the engine in a clockwise direction until the timing/top dead centre (TDC) marks align as per your manual. Ensure you use the appropriate mark.

Valve clearances are usually checked with the engine at TDC on its compression stroke, so that the valves are closed and a small clearance can be felt at each rocker arm. If the engine is not on its compression stroke, rotate the crankshaft clockwise one full turn (360°) so that the timing/TDC marks once again align.

Insert a feeler gauge that's the same thickness as the correct valve clearance as specified in your manual between the rocker arm and stem of each valve, and check that it is a firm sliding fit – you should feel a slight drag when the you pull the gauge out.

If the valve clearance is too small or too large, slacken the locknut and turn the adjuster until a firm sliding fit is obtained, then tighten the locknut securely, making sure the adjuster does not turn as you do so. Re-check the clearances.

Apply some engine oil to the valve assemblies, rockers and camshaft before installing the valve cover and fit a new cover gasket or O-ring. Install the remaining components in the reverse order of removal.

Variator and clutch – check and lubrication

Variator

Remove the drive pulley and the variator as instructed in your manual. Disassemble the variator and check all components for wear as described in your manual. If applicable, grease the rollers and the roller tracks in the housing.

Clutch and pulleys

Remove the clutch(es) and pulley assemblies as described in your manual. Take apart the pulley assembly and check all the components as described in your manual, paying particular attention to the bearing surfaces of the inner and outer pulley halves, and the condition of the bearings.

Wheels and tyres – general check

Wheels

Cast wheels are virtually maintenance free, but they should be kept clean and checked periodically for cracks and other damage. Also check the wheel runout and alignment. Sometimes damaged cast wheels can be professionally repaired, but often replacement is the only safe option.

Check the rubber bodies of valves for damage and deterioration, and have them renewed as necessary. Also, make sure the valve cap is in place and tight. If fitted, check that the wheel balance weights are firmly and securely attached to the rims.

Tyres

Check the tyre condition and tread depth as per the daily (pre-ride) checks.

Don't be daunted by mechanical assemblies. Do things by the book (workshop manual) and it will be fine

Brakes

Care for your scooter's braking
system comes high on the
maintenance schedule for
obvious reasons. Scooters use
drum and disc brakes or a
combination of the two. Inspection
and maintenance are relatively
simple, but as there is a big
safety issue here, enlist expert
help for brake maintenance if you
doubt your mechanical capability
in the slightest.

On some scooters, visual inspection of brake pads is possible. On others the calipers may have to be removed

For drum brake inspection, look at the wear indicator on the drum adjacent to the operating arm. If there is no wear indicator, ensure that the arm is not making an angle of less than 90 degrees with the brake fully applied

Inspection

Because braking relies on friction, as discussed in the description of brake systems in Chapter Three, the main thing to check on either type of brake is the amount of friction material on the pads (disc brakes) or shoes (drum brakes). Every time the brakes are applied a little more friction material is lost, and if your scootering involves a lot of stop/start work pad or shoe wear can be rapid.

There's no need to remove brake calipers to check pad wear. By simply looking up into the caliper you should be able to see the wear indicators. These take the form of a groove cut across the friction material. When the groove disappears or becomes very shallow, the pad is due for replacement. On multi-disc systems, particularly where brakes are linked, pads don't wear evenly. So check all the pads and never allow them to wear down to the steel backing that the friction material is attached to or it will damage the discs. Being enclosed, visual inspection of drum brake shoes is more difficult and can sometimes require wheel removal. However most drums have external wear indicators, usually an arrow on the brake lever at the drum pointing to a wear scale cast on to the brake plate.

Remove retaining pins to allow the pads to be taken out of the caliper

With the pistons pushed back into the caliper, fit the new pads

You might struggle to get your calipers as clean as this new example, but remove as much dirt as you can using brake cleaner

Take up slack caused by wear in drum brakes by tightening the cable adjuster. Ensure that the wheel can still spin freely without binding when the brake is applied

Replacing disc brake pads

To fit new brake pads the caliper(s) will have to be removed so that the moving piston(s) can be pushed back with a piece of wood to accommodate the new pads. The pistons will have moved closer to the disc to make up for pad wear. Before doing this, clean the moving piston(s) as thoroughly as you can. If pistons are pushed back without doing this, dirt and brake dust can be forced back into the caliper, preventing the pistons withdrawing properly when the brake lever is released. A generous squirt of brake cleaner and a wipe with a rag is usually enough to clean the piston(s). More stubborn deposits can be shifted with the help of an old toothbrush.

The brake fluid level will rise in the reservoir as the caliper(s) are pushed back and may have to be siphoned off with a syringe. Be careful not to get fluid on paintwork or plastics – it can attack them in seconds.

Add more brake fluid of the correct type as you pump the calipers up after refitting if required. Do not allow the fluid level to get too low while you're doing this or air can enter the system, and make sure you pump the brake lever to put the pads back in proper contact with the disc before riding.

Brake shoes

Drum brake shoe wear is gauged on most machines by a wear indicator on the outside of the brake plate. Where no such indicator is fitted, if the brake plate lever can form an angle of less than 90 degrees when the brake is applied, the shoes are due for replacement.

Replacement means removing the wheel(s), so make sure that the scooter is properly supported. Slacken off brake cables. Years ago brake shoes contained asbestos, these days modern materials are used. But it still makes sense to wear a mask where there is any danger of coming into contact with brake dust. Use a rag soaked in brake cleaner to clean out drums and check the braking surface for excessive wear or scoring. Brake shoe return springs should be in good condition and greased very lightly before they are replaced. A very light application of grease around lever pivots is a good idea too.

Other brake maintenance

As well as the pads and shoes, other elements of the braking system require attention too.

Hydraulic disc systems self adjust to compensate for pad wear, but keep an eye on the fluid level in the reservoir. If the level drops below the minimum marker on the reservoir there is again a chance that air will be drawn into the system, reducing its efficiency dramatically and making the controls feel spongy. Check the fluid level indicators regularly on the master cylinders and never let it drop below the minimum mark. If air does enter the system, the brakes will have to be bled.

Brake fluid is hygroscopic and absorbs moisture from the atmosphere over time. This impairs efficiency and makes the brakes feel spongy. Fluid should be replaced in accordance with the service intervals suggested in your manual. If no interval is suggested, replace fluid every 6,000 miles (10,000 kilometres) or every two years, whichever comes first.

As drum brake shoes wear, slack in the operating cables will have to be taken up. Check your scooter's manual for details of your system. Cables must be in good condition and kept correctly adjusted and lubricated. Too much cable free play and the shoes will not be able to make full contact with the drum; too little and there is a danger that the brake will bind. Keep brake operating lever pivot points on drum brakes greased, but be careful not to use so much grease that some might contaminate the shoes or braking surfaces or attract abrasive dirt. A dry film lubricant is preferable.

Disc and drum surfaces need to be checked regularly too. Discs should be inspected for cracks, as should drums. Discs and drums should also be measured for wear and distortion, and replaced if necessary. The minimum thicknesses are normally stamped on the parts, and can also be found in your manual along with maximum permissible run out.

On disc brake systems the hydraulic seals and hoses degrade over time and must be renewed in accordance with your scooter's service schedule. Again, if no interval is suggested replace hoses every 12,000 miles (20,000 kilometres) or three years, whichever comes first. Inspect hoses and unions regularly for signs of leaks and corrosion at the banjos.

Some scooter brake systems have cable operated hydraulics. In the case of these, apart from periodic attention to the hydraulics, free play will have to be taken out of the cable as it stretches with use.

Once brakes are reassembled double check tightness of caliper mounting bolts, and pump the brake lever a few times to put the pads back in contact with the discs

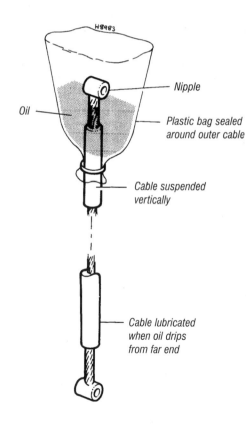

Nipple

Oil

Plastic bag sealed around outer cable

Cable suspended vertically

Cable lubricated when oil drips from far end

Home made cable oiler does the job for drum brake systems where a more sophisticated oiler is unavailable

Cables

Cables perform some basic but vital duties on your scooter. They can be found operating the throttle, the oil pump on two-strokes, the choke and driving the speedo. And apart from all-hydraulic systems, they operate the brakes, too.

Simple as cables are, they do require some care and attention for optimum performance. The most common problem is chaffing where the cable flexes with the steering or rubs on the bodywork or similar, wearing through the outer casing. Once this happens water is likely to creep in and corrosion won't be far behind.

Check for chaffing by inspecting the entire length of cables for flat spots on the outers. You should be able to see potential problems by turning the steering, or having an assistant turn it lock-to-lock and watching the cables.

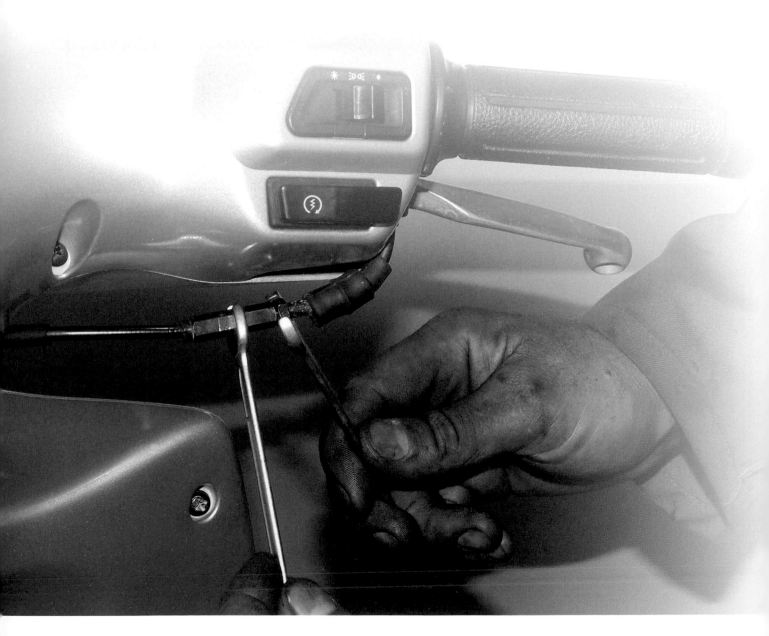

Routing

When you route cables, the straighter they are the better. Tight bends will make the cable harder to operate, increase the wear rate internally and possibly cause the cable to stick. Bad routing can also cause a cable to operate when flexed. Before replacing a cable, make a note of how the original was routed. Inadvertent operation through bad routing is particularly a problem where the throttle and brakes are concerned. If you do fit a new throttle cable always move the bars from lock to lock with the engine running to make sure the throttle doesn't operate.

Cables should also be routed away from components that build up significant amounts of heat, such as exhaust systems and engine casings, or the outers will melt and internal lubrication will be lost.

Adjustment

Cables must be correctly adjusted for proper operation of controls. There must be adequate free play between the inner and outer so that controls aren't operated inadvertently when the bars are turned or the suspension extends and compresses. For correct cable adjustment refer to your manual. Most are adjusted by simple barrel and locknut arrangements or in the case of brakes, by adjusters at the brake drum and/or lever end of the cables. Throttle cables have fine adjusters close to the twistgrip and other ones at the carb/throttle body end. Where cable-operated and relevant, they can also be found at the two-stroke oil pump. On some two-stroke scooters the oil pump and carb have to be synchronised. Refer to your manual.

Lubrication

As cables age they get harder to use. This can be caused by fraying of the internal wire, or by dirt build up in the cable. If a cable is frayed then it should be replaced immediately. If it is simply dirty, then lubricating the cable might displace some of the dirt and make it easier to use.

It is possible to lubricate cables by creating a reservoir at one end and letting gravity draw lubricant through the cable. A quicker method is to use force. You can buy an adaptor that seals itself around one end of a cable. You then connect an aerosol lubricant (not chain lube) and squirt. The pressure expels dirt and ensures the cable is fully lubricated.

Another method is to use a pressure lubricator filled with light oil and operated by hand to force the oil through the cable.

If an cable outer has a nylon liner, don't use oil to lubricate it. Oil can make the liner swell and cause the cable to seize. Use a silicone spray instead.

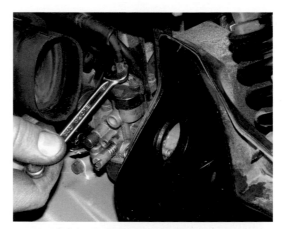

Taking up the slack in a throttle cable at the carburettor end. Take care not to take up so much that the idle rises or the throttle can be operated when the bars are moved from side to side

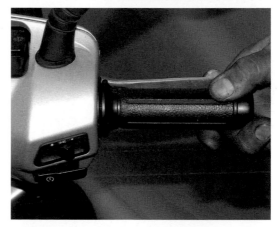

Checking throttle freeplay at the handlebar end. Throttle action should be smooth and should willingly snap shut when released

Pressure lubricator forces light oil in between the cable inner and outer

Aerosol adaptor cable lubricator makes oiling control cables a quick, easy and clean job

Bearings

Unlike engine bearings, which, all things being correct, have a ready supply of fresh injected or circulated lubricant to take care of them, chassis bearings do not, so require regular attention and lubrication.

Checking for front wheel bearing wear with the wheel off of the ground

Looking for play in the steering head bearings, again with the front wheel off of the ground

There are four sets of chassis bearings to check: wheel, swingarm, suspension linkages and bushes, and headstock.

We looked at the suspension bushes and bearings when we talked about suspension maintenance so we'll concentrate on wheel and headstock bearings in this section. Unlubricated, worn or badly adjusted bearings will adversely affect your scooter's handling characteristics. Fortunately checking them is a fairly simple task, especially with a friend helping.

Wheel bearings

To check the front wheel bearings you need to establish if there is any sideplay. The wheel should be free to spin forwards and backwards. To check bearings, set the steering in the straight ahead position. Have your scooter on its centrestand and have a helper lean on the back of the bike.

Grab the wheel from one side and try pulling the top towards you while pushing the bottom end away. Any clicking or clunking you perceive is likely to be in the bearings, and the wheel should be removed to replace them. The procedure is the same for the rear wheel; again, it's easier if the wheel is off the ground by means of the centrestand. In the case of many scooter rear wheels, there are no bearings in the wheel itself. Instead they are located in the drive shaft on which the wheel locates.

Wheel bearings are usually ball type with one pressed into each side of the hub. With prevention being better than cure, unsealed types can be repacked with grease in situ at regular intervals to prolong their life.

When fitting new bearings, drive only on the outer race to avoid damage, and ensure they are going in square to avoid damaging their housings.

Transmission bearings

Rough power delivery and suspicious noises from the transmission can often be traced to failing bearings or bushes. There is a variety in the drive train for the input and output shafts, the clutch and the pulleys. Refer to your workshop manual for replacement methods.

Swingarm bushes

Checking the swingarm pivot bushes is a similar procedure to wheel bearings. You need to try to move the swingarm from side to side with the scooter on its centrestand. If the bushes feel suspect, you can carry out the same test to make doubly sure with the suspension disconnected from the swingarm. But in order to do this the scooter will have to be on either a centrestand, a stand under the scooter or suspended from a beam in the workshop. It's much easier to feel swingarm pivot bearing play this way.

Scooter swingarms usually have bushes although there may be other types of bearing found on super scooters. Refer to your manual for information on replacement.

Steering bearings

Headstock, or steering, bearings need to be checked in two ways. With no weight on the front wheel move the bars left to right. Steering action should be smooth and light. Any notchiness or tight spots are signs of bearing damage, and they should be replaced.

Because of the hard work these bearings do they often work loose. Still with no weight on the front, get someone to push and pull quite hard on the bottom of the front suspension. While they do this, check for small movement by placing your fingers behind the top of the steering stem where the handlebars attach. If you feel movement, the bearings are loose and need adjusting, which your manual will explain how to do. You can also check for free play by pushing and pulling at the bottom of the front suspension.

Steering bearings benefit from regular regreasing and being correctly adjusted. The most common type on scooters are uncaged ball, although some larger machines use taper roller or caged ball. Uncaged balls can be tricky to fit, as the grease you've used to hold them in the bottom race while you get the bottom yoke back in fails to do so, and the tiny balls drop onto the workshop floor.

Using a drift to drive out a wheel bearing for inspection and possible replacement. Often driving a bearing out renders it unservicable and replacement is the only option

Checking for play in the rear wheel bearings. Again the wheel should be off of the ground. Get the scooter up on its centrestand

Use plenty of grease to hold replacement steering-head ballbearings in place

Bearing reference numbers allow you to order replacements cheaper from bearing suppliers, rather than paying the often hefty prices asked for 'official' spares

Electrical

Ensure your battery is properly strapped in to its carrier. If free to move about, the plates in the cells can be damaged

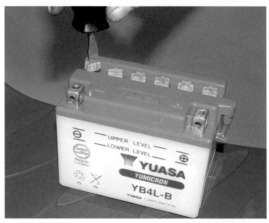

Non-maintenance free battery will require that the plugs for each cell are occasionally removed to top up with deionised water

Always remove the earth first and reconnect it last. In this case, as with most modern scooters, the earth is the negative

Modern scooter electrical systems are becoming increasingly sophisticated and efficient. This is good news in terms of functionality, but bad news from the point of view that they are less user serviceable. When those mysterious black boxes fail, the only cure is usually replacement. But a lot of problems encountered on scooters can be traced to poorly maintained batteries and wiring, so it pays to keep on top of their maintenance and check their condition regularly.

Battery

Keep an eye on your battery. Unless yours is of the maintenance-free type, you must check that it's filled to within the correct levels as indicated on the casing. If low, top it up with a little de-ionised water, but be careful not to get any acidic fluid from the battery on you, your clothes or the scooter. A battery that needs to be topped up too regularly indicates problems with the charging system. Refer to your manual for checks.

Make frequent checks to ensure that the battery terminals are tight. These can work loose and cause problems that appear to be the fault of other electrical systems, when in fact they are working just fine. A smear of petroleum jelly or electrical grease prevents corrosion forming on the terminals and ensures a good connection.

Typically a conventional lead acid battery will last for up to three years provided it is properly maintained and kept charged up using a trickle charger when the scooter isn't in regular use; expect even longer service from a sealed-for-life type.

Connectors can corrode internally. A smear of petroleum jelly or silicon grease on terminals and around the bodies where the units join will prevent this and make connectors easier to undo later

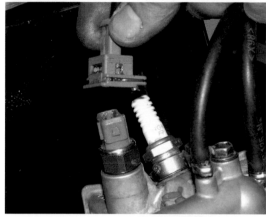

Every electrical component has a vital task to do, so regular inspection and attention as required is essential

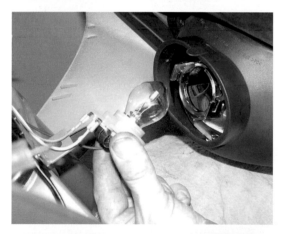

Spade type fuses are easy to access, remove and inspect. Replacement is equally easy. Ampage is clearly marked on the colour-coded fuse bodies

Connectors

Make regular checks of the push-fit connectors that wire the various electrical components into the wiring loom and on the loom itself. If even a small amount of moisture gets into the connector blocks and bullets, failures can occur. Split the connections and spray a little contact cleaner on the pins. Be careful not to spray bodywork or other plastic or painted components as they may be attacked by the contact cleaner. Plastic-friendly contact cleaners are available, and it should say on the tin or spray bottle whether or not they are.

Smearing a little bit of silicon grease or a squirt of WD40 on the connector body before reconnection will make them easier to split next time.

Bulbs

As mentioned in the daily maintenance section, check that your lights work. It's incredibly easy to forget to do this. After all, how often do you see cars at night with one or more lights out? Check head and tail lights, indicators and apply both brakes to check the brake light and its switches are working before every ride. There's a major safety issue here.

If you notice the direction indicator idiot light on the dash flashing quicker than usual, it's normally a sign that one or more of the indicator bulbs has failed.

When performing your routine checks of lights and indicators, give the horn a quick blast to make sure that's working too.

Fuses

First thing to suspect when an electrical component stops working is its fuse. Fuses or fuseboxes are usually located in easily accessible places – under the seat or bodywork or close to the battery.

There's usually a helpful key on a printed label in the lid of the fusebox to tell you which does what and sometimes there are a couple of spares too. Some machines have just a single fuse for all the systems, usually found in the feed side of the battery.

A blown fuse often indicates a short circuit or a faulty electrical component, but sometimes they just blow for no reason, especially on machines that vibrate a lot. If you replace a fuse and it blows again, the fault requires further investigation. Don't be tempted to fit a higher rated fuse or to short it out. Some scooters have resettable circuit breakers in place of main fuses.

MoTs

An MoT certificate is a legal requirement for scooters over three years old used on the road in the UK. You can't buy a tax disc without one and your insurance may be invalidated if you have an accident while your bike has no MoT.

But remember that an MoT certificate is no more than a piece of paper stating a particular scooter was in roadworthy condition at the time it was inspected. It shouldn't be taken as hard evidence of overall mechanical condition, either for the scooter you own now or when buying a second-hand one.

Here are the areas the MoT inspector will be looking at. You'll save a lot of time, hassle and money if you check them yourself before going to the test centre.

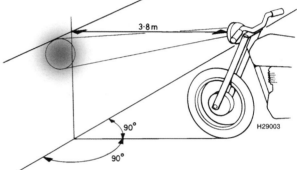

Lights, indicators, horn and reflector

- Headlight and tail light must both operate with the switch in high and low beam positions
- With the switch in the parking light position, front and tail light must light up
- Indicators must flash at the proper speed and the warning lights for them and their switch must work properly too. If your scooter has a hazard warning system, all four indicators must flash when it's operated
- The brake light must come on when each brake is operated. Scooters used after April 1, 1986, must have a brake light switch for both front and rear brakes
- Horn must have a continuous tone and sufficient volume
- Headlight beam must be at the right height. The MoT station has equipment to check this. If you think yours is out, check it as per the diagram on this page. Draw a horizontal line on the garage wall the same height as the centre of your headlight and position the scooter at the distance and angle shown in the diagram. Draw a vertical line in 'line with the centreline of the scooter. Now take the scooter off its stand and sit on it. When the headlight is dipped, the beam on the wall should fall below the horizontal and to the left of the vertical lines.

Exhaust

- Must be securely mounted and not fouling rear suspension components or wheel
- The scooter will be started and the throttle operated to ensure there are no holes or leaks in the entire system, including the collector box, where applicable
- The tester will look for either an original fitment exhaust, or the BSAU 193 stamp on the silencer. Bikes made before January 1, 1985, are exempt from this requirement. Anything marked 'race use only' or 'not for road use' will be failed. Overall loudness on questionable cans and systems generally is at the discretion of the tester.

Final drive

- The final transmission will be checked for leaks that could lead to oil getting on the rear tyre.

Steering

- The front wheel will be raised off the ground and the bars turned from lock to lock to check bars and switches don't foul bodywork or trap the rider's thumbs. Broken lockstops and poorly-fitted non-standard bars can cause problems here
- At the same time the tester will be looking for free steering movement without drag or notchiness caused by incorrectly routed cables or worn or badly adjusted head bearings
- The tester will also look for play in the head bearings by pulling on the bottom of the fork legs
- Handlebars and controls must be securely mounted, as should the grips.

Front suspension

- With the scooter off the stand, the tester will sit on it, hold the front brake on and pump the forks up and down to check they don't bind and that there's adequate damping
- Fork seals and the stanchion area next to them will be checked, the former for leaks, the latter for pitting or corrosion.

Rear suspension

- The inspector will have an assistant hold the front of the scooter while they bounce the rear with the scooter off its stand. They're looking for adequate damping in the rear shock(s) while checking nothing is fouling
- The inspector will look at the shock(s) to check the damper rod(s) aren't corroding and the damping oil isn't leaking
- The swingarm's pivot bearings will be checked by pulling it from side to side with the rear wheel raised off the ground. At the same time, the rear wheel will be pulled up by its highest point to check for wear in the suspension linkages and bushes.

Brakes

- Each wheel will be raised off the ground, the brakes operated then released and the wheel spun to check for binding
- Brake discs will be checked for cracks and to ensure they're securely mounted
- Pad material will be checked visually on disc systems to ensure the pads aren't on their wear limit
- Drum brakes will be checked for free operation of the lever and that the angle between operating cable or rod isn't too large with the brake applied
- Brake hoses and their unions will be looked at for bulging in flexible pipes and signs of corrosion and hydraulic fluid leakage elsewhere
- Rear brake torque arms will be checked to ensure they're secure and that fasteners are held on by locknuts or split pins
- ABS equipped scooters have a self-check warning light in the instrument cluster; the tester will check that this is working
- The tester will check braking efficiency, but this is nothing to worry about if you're satisfied your brakes are properly maintained.

Wheels and tyres

- Cast wheels must be free from cracks
- Rims must be uncreased and true. Wheels will be raised from the ground and spun to check the tyres and rims are true, and to make sure they don't foul mudguards or suspension components
- Wheel bearings will be checked for excessive wear. See the pages in this chapter on bearings for advice on how to check these
- Tyres will be checked for adequate tread as well as sidewall and tread condition. See the section on tyres for more information
- Tyres will also be checked to ensure they are of the correct type and match each other front and rear. Tyres must be suitable for road use, anything marked otherwise will fail the MoT. Direction arrows on the tyres will be checked too
- Security of wheel spindles is another item on the tester's agenda. Where they were fitted as standard, self-locking or catellated nuts with split or R-clips must still be present
- Wheel alignment will also be checked.

General checks

Remember, the MoT tester isn't looking to catch you out. He's simply checking that your scooter is roadworthy and safe. So apart from the items listed above, check that body panels, seat, mudguards and major fasteners are secure.

All footrests and controls must be securely mounted. Excessive corrosion of frames or load-bearing components will result in an MoT failure, so check these too.

Finally, make sure your scooter is presentable. If you wheel it through the door of the test centre with parts wired on and broken bits dragging on the floor, it's likely you'll be asked to wheel it straight out again. The better the general condition of the bike, the better your chances of an MoT pass.

Storage

Unless you're commuting to and from work on your scooter all year round, are an all-seasons recreational rider or are lucky enough to live in a sunny climate, your scooter will most likely spend a few months of the year in storage. If you want it to be in a decent state when you want to ride it again, you'll have to do more than simply parking up your scooter in the garage or shed and forgetting about it.

A scooter's exposed parts are highly susceptible to corrosion caused by road salt used to melt ice and snow in colder countries. Despite extensive bodywork on most models, it's surprising how much destructive salt and dirt can get under the panels. Corrosion can take hold in a matter of days, and it's hard to stop the rot. So give your scooter a good wash before you put it away, and make sure the machine is completely dry before it's consigned to the shed.

Remove body panels to reach the awkward places underneath. A firm-bristled bottle brush or one of the specialist brushes for motorcycle cleaning makes life easier and saves your knuckles, although using a pressure washer is perhaps the most convenient and effective method. Just remember not to be too vigorous around steering, suspension and wheel bearings, and electrical components.

A few simple precautions will ensure that your scooter is easily recommissioned after a lengthy lay-up. Don't just stick it in the shed or garage and hope

● Coat the piston bore(s) and rings with oil by removing the sparkplug(s) and squirting around a teaspoon of oil down the sparkplug hole(s). Put the plug(s) back in and crank the engine over with the kickstart (where fitted) or on the electric start with the kill switch off. Some scooters only allow the engine to turn with the kill switch on so the plug(s) will have to be earthed against the cylinder head, far enough away from the sparkplug hole(s) to avoid igniting any fuel vapour in the bore(s).

● Drain petrol from the carb(s) float bowl(s). You'll find a drain screw at the bottom of the float bowl. This prevents residual petrol in the carbs turning to varnish and blocking small carburettor orifices and airways. Most scooters have vacuum taps, but if a manual one is fitted, turn It off and allow the scooter to run until the engine stops to make sure no fuel is left in the carbs. If your scooter is going to be off the road for a long time, add fuel stabiliser to the petrol. Otherwise petrol can go off in storage and you'll need fresh stuff come spring. Or make sure the fuel tank is at least half empty before storage and top up with a healthy dose of fresh fuel come spring. Remember to dispose of old fuel properly.

● Air intakes and silencer orifices can be plugged or covered in polythene to prevent the build up of condensation. Run the scooter until it's hot, allow to cool then cover.

● Most batteries, even new ones, will discharge and go flat if a scooter isn't used for a long spell, such as over winter. The problem is even more likely to arise if your scooter is alarmed, no matter how small the drain. A trickle charger keeps batteries topped up without damaging them. It's best to remove the battery from the scooter and keep it somewhere where there's no danger of it freezing. If it's an unsealed type battery, ensure there's enough electrolyte in it.

● If the scooter is liquid-cooled, check that it contains anti-freeze. It only takes one freezing night to incur expensive damage. Corrosion inhibitors in the anti-freeze will help prevent internal damage to the cooling system.

● Consider a light coat of WD40 or similar aerosol water-repellent oil on fork sliders and other exposed metal parts. Obviously don't spray the brake discs.

● Check tyre pressures. A scooter stood for several months on flat tyres is likely to deform them so badly that they will lose their shape or split. Deflate by no more than 5–10psi. If your scooter has a centrestand, put the machine on that and place blocks of wood under each wheel to protect them from damp. Rotate the wheels periodically so they're not standing on the same section of tyre.

● Tempting as it is to start the engine every so often, try not to unless you intend to let it get up to operating temperature. If the engine isn't thoroughly warm condensation is likely to form in the engine and contaminate the oil. This can cause expensive internal corrosion.

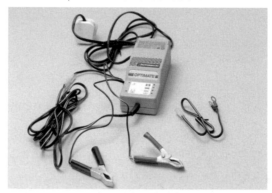

Trickle chargers keep batteries in optimum condition

Disconnect the battery while your scooter's in storage

Coat plated parts and exposed alloy with WD40 or similar. But take care not to get the oil on brake discs

Trouble Shooting

When things go wrong, as they sometimes do, don't panic. A scooter is a mechanical entity and as such is governed by rules of basic engineering and mechanics. By applying a little logic it's reasonably easy to drill down to the root of a problem, and even if your own mechanical skills or workshop resources don't stretch to it, you'll be able to point the guys in the shop in the right direction.

To help you see the trees from the forest, there follows some basic fault-finding material which will at least guide you in the right direction. Two-stroke riders can ignore any references to valves and camshafts, of course, but the rest of the material pretty much applies regardless of engine type. Remember this is a general guide, so for specific treatment of problems refer to the manual for your scooter.

Engine doesn't start or is difficult to start

Starter motor doesn't rotate

Engine kill switch OFF.
Fuse blown. Check main fuse and starter circuit fuse. See your manual.

Battery voltage low.
Check and recharge battery.

Starter motor defective.
Make sure the wiring to the starter is secure. Make sure the starter relay clicks when the start button is pushed. If the relay clicks, then the fault is in the wiring or motor.

Starter relay faulty.
See your manual.

Starter switch not contacting.
The contacts could be wet, corroded or dirty. Disassemble and clean the switch. See your manual.

Wiring open or shorted.
Check all wiring connections and harnesses to make sure that they are dry, tight and not corroded. Also check for broken or frayed wires that can cause a short to ground (earth). Refer to the wiring diagram in your manual.

Ignition (main) switch defective.
Check the switch according to the procedure in your manual. Replace the switch with a new one if it is defective.

Engine kill switch defective.
Check for wet, dirty or corroded contacts. Clean or replace the switch as necessary.

Faulty side stand switch.
Check the wiring to the switch and the switch itself according to the procedures in your manual.

Starter motor rotates but engine does not turn over

Starter clutch defective.
Inspect and repair or replace. See your manual.

Damaged idle/reduction or starter gears.
Inspect and replace the damaged parts. See your manual.

Starter works but engine won't turn over (seized).
Seized engine caused by one or more internally damaged components. Failure due to wear, abuse or lack of lubrication. Damage can include seized valves, followers, camshafts, pistons, crankshaft, connecting rod bearings, or transmission or bearings. See your manual for engine disassembly.

No fuel flow

No fuel in tank.

Fuel tank breather hose obstructed.

Fuel tap filter or in-line filter (carburettor models) or fuel pump assembly filter (fuel injection models) clogged.
Remove the tap or pump and clean or renew the filter. See your manual.

Fuel line clogged.
Pull the fuel line loose and carefully blow it through.

Float needle valve clogged (carburettor models).
For all of the valves to be clogged, either a very bad batch of fuel with an unusual additive has been used, or some other foreign material has entered the tank. Many times after a machine has been stored for many months without running, the fuel turns to a varnish-like liquid and forms deposits on the inlet needle valves and jets. The carburettor(s) should be removed and overhauled if draining the float chambers doesn't solve the problem.

Fuel pump or relay (fuel injection models) faulty.
Check the fuel pump and relay. See your manual.

Engine flooded (carburettor models).
Float height too high. See your manual.

Float needle valve worn or stuck open.
Dirt, rust or other debris can cause the valve to seat improperly, causing excess fuel to be admitted to the float chamber. In this case, the float chamber should be cleaned and the needle valve and seat inspected. If the needle and seat are worn, then the leaking will persist and the parts should be replaced.

Starting technique incorrect.

Under normal circumstances (i.e. if all the carburettor functions are sound) the machine should start with little or no throttle. When the engine is cold, the choke should be operated and the engine started without opening the throttle. When the engine is at operating temperature, only a very slight amount of throttle should be necessary. If the engine is flooded, turn the fuel tap OFF (where fitted) and hold the throttle open while cranking the engine. This will allow additional air to reach the cylinder(s). Remember to turn the fuel tap back ON after the engine starts.

Engine flooded (fuel injection models).

Faulty pressure regulator – if it is stuck closed there could be excessive pressure in the fuel rail. Check as described in your manual.

Injector(s) stuck open, allowing a constant flow of fuel into the engine.

Check as described in your manual.

Starting technique incorrect.

See advice as for carburated bikes. But remember some fuel injected scooters have no choke lever and most have no manually-operated fuel tap.

No spark or weak spark

Ignition switch OFF.

Engine kill switch turned to the OFF position.

Battery voltage low.

Check and recharge the battery as necessary. See your manual.

Spark plug(s) dirty, defective or worn out.

Locate reason for fouled plugs using spark plug condition chart and follow the plug maintenance procedures. See your manual.

Spark plug cap(s) faulty.

Check condition. Replace if cracks or deterioration are evident. See your manual.

Spark plug cap(s) not making good contact.

Make sure that the plug caps fit snugly over the plug ends.

Ignition control unit (carburettor models) or ECM (fuel injection models) defective.

Check the unit, referring to your manual for details.

Pulse generator defective.

Check the unit, referring to your manual for details.

Ignition coil(s) defective.

Check the coil(s), referring to your manual.

Ignition or kill switch shorted.

Usually caused by water, corrosion, damage or excessive wear. The switches can be disassembled and cleaned with electrical contact cleaner. If cleaning does not help, replace the switches referring to your manual.

Wiring shorted or broken between:

a) Ignition (main) switch and engine kill switch (or blown fuse)
b) Ignition control unit or ECM and engine kill switch
c) Ignition control unit or ECM and ignition coils
d) Ignition coils and spark plugs
e) Ignition control unit or ECM and pulse generator.

Make sure that all wiring connections are clean, dry and tight.

Look for chafed and broken wires.

Compression low

Spark plugs loose.

Remove the plug(s) and inspect threads. Reinstall and tighten to the specified torque. See your manual.

Cylinder head not sufficiently tightened down.

See your manual. If a cylinder head is suspected of being loose, then there's a chance that the gasket or head is damaged if the problem has persisted for any length of time.

Incorrect valve clearance (four-strokes).

Check and adjust the valve clearances as per your manual.

Cylinder and/or piston worn.

Excessive wear will cause compression pressure to leak past the rings. This is usually accompanied by worn rings as well. A top-end overhaul will be required.

Piston rings worn, weak, broken, or sticking.

Broken or sticking piston rings usually indicate a lubrication or carburation problem that causes excess carbon deposits or seizures to form on the pistons and rings. Top-end overhaul will again be necessary.

Piston ring-to-groove clearance excessive.

This is caused by excessive wear of the piston ring lands. Piston and ring replacement will be called for.

Cylinder head gasket damaged.

If a head is allowed to become loose, or if excessive carbon build-up on the piston crown and combustion chamber causes extremely high compression, the head gasket may leak. Retorquing the head is not always sufficient to restore the seal, so gasket replacement is needed too.

Cylinder head warped.

This is caused by overheating or improperly tightened head bolts. Machine shop resurfacing or head replacement and a new gasket will be needed.

Valve spring broken or weak (four-strokes).

Caused by component failure or wear; the springs must be replaced.

Valve not seating properly (four-strokes).

This is caused by a bent valve (from over-revving or improper valve adjustment), burned valve or seat (improper carburation) or an accumulation of carbon deposits on the seat (from carburation or lubrication problems). The valves must be cleaned and/or replaced and the seats serviced if possible or replaced by an engineering shop.

Stalls after starting

Improper choke action (carburettor models).

See your manual.

Ignition malfunction.

See your manual.

Carburettor or fuel injection system malfunction.

See your manual.

Fuel contaminated.

The fuel can be contaminated with either dirt or water, or can change chemically if the machine is allowed to sit for several months or more. Drain the tank and float chambers. Also check that fuel can flow freely.

Intake air leak.
Check for loose carburettor or throttle body-to-intake manifold connections, loose or missing vacuum gauge adaptor screws or hoses, or loose carburettor tops.

Engine idle speed incorrect.
Turn idle adjusting screw until the engine idles at the specified rpm in your manual. On fuel injection models, check other components as specified in your manual.

Rough idle

Ignition malfunction.
See your manual.

Idle speed incorrect.
See your manual.

Carburettors or throttle bodies not synchronised (multi cylinder machines).
Adjust with vacuum gauge or manometer set as described in your manual.

Carburettor or throttle body or fuel injection system malfunction.
See your manual.

Fuel contaminated.
The fuel can be contaminated with either dirt or water, or can change chemically if the machine is allowed to sit for several months or more. Drain the tank and float chambers as per your manual.

Intake air leak.
Check for loose carburettor or throttle body-to-intake manifold connections, loose or missing vacuum gauge adaptor screws or hoses, or loose carburettor tops.

Air filter clogged.
Clean or replace the air filter element.

Poor running at low speeds

Spark weak

Battery voltage low.
Check and recharge battery.

Spark plug(s) fouled, defective or worn out.

Spark plug cap defective.
See your manual.

Spark plug cap(s) not making contact.

Incorrect spark plug(s).
Wrong type, heat range or cap configuration. Check and install correct plugs.

Ignition control unit (carburettor models) or ECM (fuel injection models) defective.
Check as per instructions in your manual.

Pulse generator defective.

Ignition coils defective.

Fuel/air mixture incorrect Carburettor models

Pilot screw(s) out of adjustment.
See your manual.

Pilot jet or air passage clogged.
Remove and overhaul the carburettors. See your manual.

Air bleed holes clogged.

Remove carburettor and blow out all passages. See your manual.

Fuel level too high or too low.
Check the float height as detailed in your manual.

Carburettor intake manifolds loose.
Check for cracks, breaks, tears or loose clamps. Replace rubber intake manifold joints if split or perished.

Fuel/air mixture incorrect Fuel injection models

Fuel injection system malfunction.
See your manual.

Fuel injector clogged.
See your manual.

Fuel pump or pressure regulator faulty.

Throttle body intake manifolds loose.
Check for cracks, breaks, tears or loose clamps. Replace rubber intake manifold joints if split or perished.

Fuel/air mixture incorrect All models

Air filter clogged, poorly sealed or missing.

Air filter housing poorly sealed.
Look for cracks, holes or loose clamps and replace or repair defective parts.

Fuel tank breather hose obstructed.

Compression low

Spark plug(s) loose.
Remove the plugs and inspect their threads. Reinstall and tighten to the specified torque in your manual.

Cylinder head not sufficiently tightened down.
If a cylinder head is suspected of being loose, then there's a chance that the gasket and head are damaged if the problem has persisted for any length of time. The head bolts should be tightened to the proper torque in the correct sequence described in your manual.

Incorrect valve clearance (four-strokes).
This means that the valve is not closing completely and compression pressure is leaking past the valve. Check and adjust the valve clearances.

Cylinder and/or piston worn.
Excessive wear will cause compression pressure to leak past the rings. This is usually accompanied by worn rings as well. A top end overhaul is necessary.

Piston rings worn, weak, broken, or sticking.
Broken or sticking piston rings usually indicate a lubrication or carburation problem that causes excess carbon deposits or seizures to form on the pistons and rings. Top-end overhaul is necessary.

Piston ring-to-groove clearance excessive.
This is caused by excessive wear of the piston ring lands. Piston and probably ring replacement is necessary.

Cylinder head gasket damaged.
If a head is allowed to become loose, or if excessive carbon build-up on the piston crown and combustion chamber causes extremely high compression, the head gasket may leak. Retorquing the head does not always restore the seal, so gasket replacement is necessary.

Cylinder head warped.
This is caused by overheating or improperly tightened head bolts. Machine shop resurfacing or head replacement is necessary.

Valve spring broken or weak (four-strokes).
Caused by component failure or wear; the springs must be replaced.

Valve not seating properly (four-strokes).
This is caused by a bent valve (from over-revving or improper valve adjustment), burned valve or seat (improper carburation) or an accumulation of carbon deposits on the seat (from carburation, lubrication problems). The valves must be cleaned and/or replaced and the seats recut or replaced if possible.

Poor acceleration

Carburettor(s) or throttle body(ies) leaking or dirty.
Overhaul them.

Fuel injection system malfunction.
Faulty fuel pump, or pressure regulator (fuel injection models).

Timing not advancing.
The pulse generator or the ignition control unit or ECM may be defective. If so, they must be replaced with new ones, as they can't be repaired.

Carburettors or throttle bodies not synchronised (multis).
Adjust them with a vacuum gauge set or manometer.

Engine oil viscosity too high.
Using a heavier oil than that recommended can damage the oil pump or lubrication system and cause drag on the engine.

Brakes dragging.
Usually caused by debris which has entered the brake piston seals, or from a warped disc or bent wheel spindle. Repair and replace as necessary.

Poor running or no power at high speed

Firing incorrect

Air filter restricted.
Clean or replace filter.

Spark plug(s) fouled, defective or worn out.

Spark plug cap(s) defective.

Spark plug cap(s) not in good contact.

Incorrect spark plug(s).
Wrong type, heat range or cap configuration. Check and install correct plugs listed in your manual.

Ignition control unit or ECM defective.

Ignition coil(s) defective.

Fuel/air mixture incorrect Carburettor models

Main jet clogged.
Dirt, water or other contaminants can clog the main jets. Clean the fuel tap filter, the in-line filter, the float

chamber area, and the jets and carburettor orifices.

Main jet wrong size.
The standard jetting is for sea level atmospheric pressure and oxygen content.

Throttle shaft-to-carb body clearance excessive.
Check manual for inspection and renewal.

Air bleed holes clogged.
Remove carburettor and blow out all passages.

Fuel level too high or too low.
Check the float height.

Carburettor intake manifold(s) loose.
Check for cracks, breaks, tears or loose clamps. Replace rubber intake manifold joints if split or perished.

Fuel pump, where fitted, faulty.

Fuel/air mixture incorrect Fuel injection models

Fuel injection system malfunction.

Fuel injector clogged.

Fuel pump or pressure regulator faulty.

Throttle body intake manifolds loose.
Check for cracks, breaks, tears or loose clamps. Replace rubber intake manifold joints if split or perished.

Fuel/air mixture incorrect All models

Air filter clogged, poorly sealed or missing.

Air filter housing poorly sealed.
Look for cracks, holes or loose clamps and replace or repair defective parts.

Fuel tank breather hose obstructed.

Compression low

Spark plug(s) loose.
Remove the plugs and inspect their threads. Reinstall and tighten to the specified torque.

Cylinder head not sufficiently tightened down.
If a cylinder head is suspected of being loose, then there's a chance that the gasket and head are damaged if the problem has persisted for any length of time. The head bolts should be tightened to the proper torque in the correct sequence.

Incorrect valve clearance (four-strokes).
This means that the valve is not closing completely and compression pressure is leaking past the valve. Check and adjust the valve clearances.

Cylinder and/or piston worn.
Excessive wear will cause compression pressure to leak past the rings. This is usually accompanied by worn rings. A top-end overhaul is necessary.

Piston rings worn, weak, broken, or sticking.
Broken or sticking piston rings usually indicate a lubrication or carburation problem that causes excess carbon deposits or seizures to form on the pistons and rings. Top-end overhaul is necessary.

Piston ring-to-groove clearance excessive.
This is caused by excessive wear of the piston ring lands. Piston and probably ring replacement is necessary.

Cylinder head gasket damaged.
If a head is allowed to become loose, or if excessive carbon build-up on the piston crown and combustion chamber causes extremely high compression, the head gasket may leak. Retorquing the head is not always sufficient to restore the seal, so gasket replacement is necessary.

Cylinder head warped.
This is caused by overheating or improperly tightened head bolts. Machine shop resurfacing or head replacement is necessary.

Valve spring broken or weak (four-strokes).
Caused by component failure or wear; the springs must be replaced.

Valve not seating properly (four-strokes).
This is caused by a bent valve (from over-revving or improper valve adjustment), burned valve or seat (improper carburation) or an accumulation of carbon deposits on the seat (from carburation or lubrication problems). The valves must be cleaned and/or replaced and the seats serviced or replaced if possible.

Knocking or pinking

Carbon build-up in combustion chamber.
Use of a fuel additive that will dissolve the adhesive bonding the carbon particles to the crown and chamber is the easiest way to remove the build-up. Otherwise, the cylinder head will have to be removed and decarbonised. Rare with modern fuels.

Incorrect or poor quality fuel.
Old or improper grades of fuel can cause detonation. This causes the piston to rattle, thus the knocking or pinging sound. Drain old fuel and always use the recommended fuel grade.

Spark plug heat range incorrect.
Uncontrolled detonation indicates the plug heat range is too hot. The plug in effect becomes a glow plug, raising cylinder temperatures. Install the proper heat range plug.

Improper air/fuel mixture.
This will cause the cylinders to run hot, which leads to detonation. Clogged jets or an air leak can cause this imbalance.

Miscellaneous causes

Throttle valve doesn't open fully.
Adjust the throttle grip freeplay.

Clutch slipping, drive belt worn or speed governor faulty.

Timing not advancing
Faulty ignition control unit or ECM.

Engine oil viscosity too high.
Using a heavier oil than recommended can damage the oil pump or lubrication system and cause drag on the engine.

Brakes dragging.
Usually caused by debris which has entered the brake piston seals, or from a warped disc or bent axle. Repair and replace as necessary.

Overheating

Engine overheats
Liquid-cooled engines

Coolant level low.
Check and add coolant.

Leak in cooling system.
Check cooling system hoses and radiator for leaks and other damage. Repair or replace parts as necessary.

Thermostat sticking open or closed.
Check and replace.

Faulty radiator cap.
Remove the cap and have it pressure tested.

Coolant passages clogged.
Have the entire system drained and flushed, then refill with fresh coolant.

Water pump defective.
Remove the pump and check the components.

Clogged radiator fins.
Clean them by blowing compressed air through the fins in the reverse direction of airflow.

Cooling fan or fan switch fault.

Air-cooled engines

Cooling ducts blocked or incorrectly fitted.

Problem with cooling fan.

Firing incorrect

Spark plug(s) fouled, defective or worn out.

Incorrect spark plug(s).

Ignition control unit or ECM defective.

Pulse generator faulty.

Faulty ignition coils.

Fuel/air mixture incorrect
Carburettor models

Main jet clogged.
Dirt, water or other contaminants can clog the main jets. Clean the fuel tap filter, the in-line filter, the float chamber area, and the jets and carburettor orifices.

Main jet wrong size.
The standard jetting is for sea level atmospheric pressure and oxygen content.

Throttle shaft-to-carburettor body clearance excessive.

Air bleed holes clogged.
Remove carburettor and blow out all passages.

Fuel level too high or too low.
Check the float height.

Carburettor intake manifolds loose.
Check for cracks, breaks, tears or loose clamps. Replace rubber intake manifold joints if split or perished.

Fuel pump faulty.

Fuel/air mixture incorrect
Fuel injection models

Fuel injection system malfunction.

Fuel injector clogged.

Fuel pump or pressure regulator faulty.

Throttle body intake manifolds loose.
Check for cracks, breaks, tears or loose clamps.
Replace rubber intake manifold joints if split or perished.

Fuel/air mixture incorrect
All models

Air filter clogged, poorly sealed or missing.

Air filter housing poorly sealed.
Look for cracks, holes or loose clamps and replace or
repair defective parts.

Fuel tank breather hose obstructed.

Compression too high

Carbon build-up in combustion chamber.
Use of a fuel additive that will dissolve the adhesive
bonding the carbon particles to the piston crown and
chamber is the easiest way to remove the build-up.
Otherwise, the cylinder head will have to be removed
and decarbonised.

**Improperly machined head surface or installation
of incorrect gasket during engine assembly.**

Engine load excessive

**Clutch slipping, drive belt worn or speed
governor faulty.**
Can be caused by damaged, loose or worn clutch
components. Refer to your manual for overhaul
procedures.

Engine oil level too high.
The addition of too much oil will cause pressurisation of
the crankcase and inefficient engine operation. Check
specifications and drain to proper level.

Engine oil viscosity too high.
Using a heavier oil than recommended can damage the
oil pump or lubrication system as well as cause drag on
the engine.

Brakes dragging.
Usually caused by debris which has entered the brake
piston seals, or from a warped disc or bent axle. Repair
and replace as necessary.

Lubrication inadequate

Oil pump out of adjustment (two-strokes)

Engine oil level too low (four-strokes)
Friction caused by intermittent lack of lubrication or from
oil that is overworked can cause overheating. The oil
provides a definite cooling function in the engine. Check
the oil level.

**Poor quality engine oil or incorrect viscosity or
type.**
Oil is rated not only according to viscosity but also
according to type. Some oils are not rated high enough
for use in this engine. Check the specifications section
in your manual and change to the correct oil.

Miscellaneous causes

Modification to exhaust system.
Most aftermarket exhaust systems cause the engine to
run leaner, which makes them run hotter. When installing
an accessory exhaust system, always rejet the
carburettors or tweak the fuel injection by means of an
aftermarket black box

Transmission problems

No drive to rear wheel

Drive belt broken or slipping.

Clutch not engaging.

Clutch friction material or drum excessively worn.

Transmission noise or vibration

Bearings or shafts worn.
Overhaul transmission

Gears worn or chipped.

Clutch drum worn unevenly.

Clutch pulley or variator pulley out of alignment.

Bent or damaged transmission shaft.

Loose clutch or variator nut.

Poor performance

Variator rollers worn or insufficiently greased.

Weak or broken clutch pulley spring.

Clutch or drum excessively worn.

Grease on clutch friction material.

Drive belt excessively worn.

Clutch not disengaging completely.

Weak or broken clutch springs.

Engine idle speed too high.

Abnormal engine noise

Knocking or pinking

Carbon build-up in combustion chamber.
Use of a fuel additive that will dissolve the adhesive
bonding the carbon particles to the piston crown and
chamber is the easiest way to remove the build-up.
Otherwise, the cylinder head will have to be removed
and decarbonised. Rare with modern fuels.

Incorrect or poor quality fuel.
Old or improper fuel can cause detonation. This causes the
pistons to rattle, thus the knocking or pinging sound. Drain
the old fuel and always use the recommended grade.

Spark plug heat range incorrect.
Uncontrolled detonation indicates that the plug heat
range is too hot. The plug in effect becomes a glow
plug, raising cylinder temperatures. Install the proper
heat range plug.

Improper fuel/air mixture.
This will cause the cylinders to run hot and lead to
detonation. Clogged jets or an air leak can cause this
imbalance.

Piston slap or rattling

Cylinder-to-piston clearance excessive.
Caused by improper assembly. Inspect and overhaul top-end parts.

Connecting rod bent.
Caused by over-revving, trying to start a badly flooded engine or from ingesting a foreign object into the combustion chamber. Replace the damaged parts.

Piston pin or piston pin bore worn or seized from wear or lack of lubrication.
Replace damaged parts.

Piston rings worn, broken or sticking.
Overhaul the top-end.

Piston seizure damage.
Usually from lack of lubrication or overheating. Replace the piston(s) and have the cylinder(s) rebored as necessary.

Connecting rod upper or lower end clearance excessive.
Caused by excessive wear or lack of lubrication. Replace worn parts.

Valve noise (four-strokes)

Incorrect valve clearances.
Adjust the clearances.

Valve spring broken or weak.
Check and replace weak valve springs.

Camshaft or cylinder head worn or damaged.
Lack of lubrication at high rpm is usually the cause of damage. Insufficient oil or failure to change the oil at the recommended intervals are the chief causes.

Other noise

Cylinder head gasket leaking.

Exhaust pipe leaking at cylinder head connection.
Caused by improper fit of pipe(s) or loose exhaust flange. All exhaust fasteners should be tightened evenly and carefully. Failure to do this will lead to a leak.

Crankshaft runout excessive.
Caused by a bent crankshaft (from over-revving) or damage from an upper cylinder component failure. Can also be attributed to dropping the machine on either of the crankshaft ends.

Engine mounting bolts loose.
Tighten all engine mount bolts.

Crankshaft bearings worn.

Camshaft drive assembly defective.

Transmission noise

Bearings worn.
Also includes the possibility that the shafts are worn. Overhaul the transmission.

Gears worn or chipped.

Metal chips jammed in gear teeth.
Probably pieces from a broken clutch, gear or shift mechanism that were picked up by the gears. This will cause early bearing failure.

Engine oil level too low.

Abnormal frame and suspension noise

Front end noise

Low fluid level or improper viscosity oil in forks.
This can sound like spurting and is usually accompanied by irregular fork action.

Spring weak or broken.
Makes a clicking or scraping sound. Fork oil, when drained, will have a lot of metal particles in it.

Steering head bearings loose or damaged.
Clicks when braking. Check and adjust or replace as necessary.

Fork yokes loose.
Make sure all clamp pinch bolts are tightened to the specified torque.

Fork tube bent.
Good possibility if machine has been dropped. Replace tube with a new one.

Front axle bolt or axle clamp bolts loose.
Tighten them to the specified torque.

Loose or worn wheel bearings.
Check and replace as needed.

Shock absorber noise

Fluid level incorrect.
Indicates a leak caused by defective seal. Shock will be covered with oil. Replace shock or seek advice on repair.

Defective shock absorber with internal damage.
This is in the body of the shock and can't be remedied. The shock must be replaced with a new one.

Bent or damaged shock body.
Replace the shock with a new one.

Loose or worn suspension linkage or swingarm components.
Check and replace as necessary.

Brake noise

Squeal caused by pad shim not installed or positioned correctly (where fitted).

Squeal caused by dust on brake pads.
Usually found in combination with glazed pads. Clean using brake cleaning solvent.

Contamination of brake pads.
Oil, brake fluid or dirt causing brake to chatter or squeal. Clean or replace pads.

Pads glazed. Caused by excessive heat from prolonged use or from contamination.
Do not use sandpaper, emery cloth, carborundum cloth or any other abrasive to roughen the pad surfaces as abrasives will stay in the pad material and damage the disc. A very fine flat file can be used, but pad replacement is suggested as a cure.

Disc warped.
Can cause a chattering, clicking or intermittent squeal. Usually accompanied by a pulsating lever and uneven braking. Replace the disc.

Loose or worn wheel bearings.
Check and replace as required.

Oil pressure indicator (four-strokes) light comes on

Engine lubrication system

Engine oil pump defective, blocked oil strainer gauze or failed relief valve.
Carry out oil pressure check as per manual.

Engine oil level low.
Inspect for leak or other problem causing low oil level and add recommended oil.

Engine oil viscosity too low.
Very old, thin oil or an improper weight of oil used in the engine. Change to correct oil.

Camshaft or journals worn.
Excessive wear causing drop in oil pressure. Replace cam and/or cylinder head. Abnormal wear could be caused by oil starvation at high rpm from low oil level or improper weight or type of oil.

Crankshaft and/or bearings worn.
Same problems as above. Check and replace crankshaft and/or bearings.

Electrical system

Oil pressure switch defective.
Check the switch according to the procedure in your manual. Replace it if it is defective.

Oil pressure indicator light circuit defective.
Check for pinched, shorted, disconnected or damaged wiring.

Excessive exhaust smoke

White smoke

Piston oil ring worn.
The ring may be broken or damaged, causing oil from the crankcase to be pulled past the piston into the combustion chamber. Replace the rings with new ones.

Cylinder(s) worn, cracked, or scored.
Caused by overheating or oil starvation. The cylinders will have to be rebored and new pistons installed.

Valve oil seal damaged or worn.
Replace oil seals with new ones.

Valve guide worn.
Perform, or have performed, a complete valve job.

Engine oil level too high, which causes the oil to be forced past the rings.
Drain oil to the proper level.

Head gasket broken between oil return and cylinder.
Causes oil to be pulled into the combustion chamber. Replace the head gasket and check the head for warpage.

Abnormal crankcase pressurisation, which forces oil past the rings.
Clogged breather is usually the cause.

Black smoke
Carburettor models

Main jet too large or loose.
Compare the jet size to the specifications in your manual.

Choke cable or linkage shaft stuck, causing fuel to be pulled through choke circuit.

Fuel level too high.
Check and adjust the float height(s) as necessary.

Float needle valve held off needle seat.
Clean the float chambers and fuel line and replace the needles and seats if necessary.

Black smoke
Fuel injection models

Fuel injection system malfunction.

Black smoke
All models

Air filter clogged.

Brown smoke
Carburettor models

Main jet too small or clogged.
Lean condition caused by wrong size main jet or by a restricted orifice. Clean float chambers and jets and compare jet size to specifications in your manual.

Fuel flow insufficient.
Float needle valve stuck closed due to chemical reaction with old fuel. Float height incorrect. Restricted fuel line. Clean line and float chamber and adjust floats if necessary.

Carburettor intake manifold clamps loose.
Faulty fuel pump.

Brown smoke
Fuel injection models

Fuel injection system malfunction.
Faulty fuel pump or pressure regulator.

Brown smoke
All models

Air filter poorly sealed or not installed.

Poor handling or stability

Handlebar hard to turn

Steering head bearing adjuster nut too tight.
Check adjustment as described in your manual.

Bearings damaged.
Roughness can be felt as the bars are turned from side-to-side. Replace bearings and races.

Races dented or worn.
Denting results from wear in only one position (e.g. straight ahead), from a collision or hitting a pothole or

from dropping the machine. Replace races and bearings. Steering stem lubrication inadequate. Causes are grease getting hard from age or being washed out by high pressure car washes. Disassemble steering head and repack and/or replace bearings.

Steering stem bent.
Caused by a collision, hitting a pothole or by dropping the machine. Replace damaged part. Don't try to straighten the steering stem.

Front tyre air pressure too low.

Handlebar shakes or vibrates excessively

Tyres worn, out of balance or at incorrect pressures.
Swingarm bearings worn.
Replace worn bearings.

Wheel rim(s) warped or damaged.
Inspect wheels for runout.

Wheel bearings worn.
Worn front or rear wheel bearings can cause poor tracking. Worn front bearings will cause wobble.

Handlebar clamp bolts loose.

Fork yoke bolts loose.
Tighten them to the specified torque in your manual.

Engine mounting bolts loose.
Will cause excessive vibration with increased engine rpm.

Handlebar pulls to one side

Frame bent.
Definitely suspect this if the machine has been dropped. May or may not be accompanied by cracking near the bend. Replace the frame if it can't be safely straightened.

Wheels out of alignment.
Caused by improper location of spindle spacers or from bent steering stem or frame.

Swingarm bent or twisted.
Caused by age (metal fatigue) or impact damage. Replace the arm.

Steering stem bent.
Caused by impact damage or by dropping the motorcycle. Replace the steering stem.

Fork tube bent.
Disassemble the forks and replace the damaged parts.

Fork oil level uneven.
Check and add or drain as necessary.

Poor shock absorbing qualities

Too hard:
a) Fork oil level excessive.
b) Fork oil viscosity too high. Use a lighter oil (see the specifications in your manual).
c) Fork tube bent. Causes a harsh, sticking feeling.
d) Shock shaft or body bent or damaged.
e) Fork internal damage.
f) Shock internal damage.
g) Tyre pressure too high.
h) Suspension adjusters incorrectly set.

Too soft:
a) Fork or shock oil insufficient and/or leaking.
b) Fork oil level too low.
c) Fork oil viscosity too light.
d) Fork springs weak or broken.
e) Shock internal damage or leakage.
f) Suspension adjusters incorrectly set.

Braking problems

Brakes are spongy, or lack power

Air in brake line.
Caused by inattention to master cylinder fluid level or by leakage. Locate problem and bleed brakes. Cable problem on drum brakes.

Pad or disc (or drum/shoes) worn.

Brake fluid leak.

Contaminated pads/shoes.
Caused by contamination with oil, grease, brake fluid, etc. Clean or replace. Clean disc/drum thoroughly with brake cleaner.

Brake fluid deteriorated.
Fluid is old or contaminated. Drain system, replenish with new fluid and bleed the system.

Master cylinder internal parts worn or damaged causing fluid to bypass.

Master cylinder bore scratched by foreign material or broken spring.
Repair or replace master cylinder.

Disc warped/drum out of true.
Replace disc/drum.

Brake lever or pedal pulsates

Disc warped/drum out of true.
Replace/skim.

Spindle bent.
Replace spindle.

Brake caliper bolts loose.

Brake caliper sliders damaged or sticking (rear caliper), causing caliper to bind.
Lubricate the sliders or replace them if they are corroded or bent.

Wheel warped or otherwise damaged.

Wheel bearings damaged or worn.

Brakes drag

Master cylinder piston seized.
Caused by wear or damage to piston or cylinder bore. Incorrect cable/rod/shoe adjustment on drum systems.

Lever sticky or stuck.
Check pivot and lubricate.

Brake caliper binds on bracket (rear caliper).
Caused by inadequate lubrication or damage to caliper sliders.

Brake caliper piston seized in bore.
Caused by wear or ingestion of dirt past deteriorated seal.

Brake pad/shoe damaged.
Pad/shoe material separated from backing plate. Usually

caused by faulty manufacturing process or from contact with chemicals. Replace.

Pads/shoes improperly installed.

Electrical problems

Battery dead or weak

Battery faulty.
Caused by sulphated plates which are shorted through sedimentation. Also, broken battery terminal making only occasional contact.

Battery cables making poor contact.

Load excessive.
Caused by addition of high wattage lights or other electrical accessories.

Ignition (main) switch defective.
Switch either grounds (earths) internally or fails to shut off system. Replace the switch.

Regulator/rectifier defective.

Alternator stator coil open or shorted.

Wiring faulty.
Wiring grounded (earthed) or connections loose in ignition, charging or lighting circuits.

Battery overcharged

Regulator/rectifier defective.
Overcharging is noticed when battery gets excessively warm.

Battery defective.
Replace battery with a new one.

Battery amperage too low, wrong type or size.
Install manufacturer's specified amp-hour battery to handle charging load.

Glossary

A

Accelerator pump A carburettor device for temporarily increasing the amount of fuel.

Air filter Either a paper, fabric, felt, foam or gauze element through which the engine draws its air.

Air/fuel ratio Proportions in which air and fuel are mixed to form a combustible gas.

Alternator A generator of alternating current (a.c.) electricity.

ABS (Anti-lock braking system) A system that prevents the wheels locking up under braking.

Ampere-hour (Ah) Measure of battery capacity.

Antifreeze A substance (usually ethylene glycol) mixed with water, and added to the cooling system, to prevent freezing of the coolant in winter.

Anti-dive System attached to the fork lower leg (slider) to prevent fork dive when braking hard.

Aspect ratio With a tyre, the ratio of the section's depth to its width.

ATF Automatic Transmission Fluid. Often used in front forks.

Axle A shaft on which a wheel revolves. Also known as a spindle.

B

Backlash The amount of movement between meshed components. Usually applies to gear teeth.

Ball bearing A bearing consisting of a hardened inner and outer race with hardened steel balls between the two races.

BDC Bottom Dead Centre – denotes that the piston is at the lowest point of its stroke in the cylinder.

Bearings Used between two working surfaces to prevent wear of the components and a build-up of heat.

Belt drive Drive by a belt. Typical applications are for drive to the camshafts and transmission, and to the rear wheel.

Bevel gear Gear with slanted teeth, a pair of such gears turning the drive through ninety degrees.

BHP Brake horsepower.

Bias-belted tyre Similar construction to radial tyre, but with outer belt running at an angle to the wheel rim.

Big-end The larger end of a connecting rod and the one mounted on the crankpin.

Bleeding The process of removing air from an hydraulic system.

Bore Diameter of a cylinder.

Bore:stroke ratio The ratio of cylinder diameter to stroke. When these are equal the engine is said to be square.

Bottom Dead Centre (BDC) Lowest point of piston's stroke in the cylinder.

Bottom-end An engine's crankcase components and all components contained there-in.

BTDC Before Top Dead Centre in terms of piston position. Ignition timing is often expressed in terms of degrees or millimetres BTDC.

Bush A cylindrical metal and/or rubber component used between two moving parts.

C

Caliper In an hydraulic brake system, the component spanning the disc and housing the pistons and brake pads.

Cam chain The chain which takes drive from the crankshaft to the camshaft(s).

Cam follower A component in contact with the camshaft lobes, transmitting motion to the valve gear.

Camshaft A rotary shaft for the operation of valve gear in poppet valve engines.

Carburettor Mixes variable volumes of air and fuel in the correct ratio.

Catalytic converter A device in the exhaust system of some machines which converts certain pollutants in the exhaust gases into less harmful substances.

Centrifugal To be thrown outwards. An outward force on an object moving around a point.

Charging system Description of the components which charge the battery.

Clutch A device for engaging or disengaging the engine from the driving wheel.

Coil spring A spiral of elastic steel.

Compression Squeezing smaller, particularly a fresh charge of mixture in the cylinder by the rising piston.

Compression damping Controls the speed the suspension compresses when hitting a bump.

Compression ratio The extent to which the contents of the cylinder are compressed by the rising piston.

Concentric Tending to a common centre.

Connecting-rod The rod connecting the piston to the crankshaft via the big and small ends.

Constant rate A spring is this when each equal increment in load produces an equal change in length. (Contrast with multi-rate and progressive rate.)

Crankcase The chamber which carries the crankshaft.

Crankshaft A forged component, using the principle of the eccentric (crank) for converting the reciprocating piston engine's linear power pulse into rotary motion.

Cross-ply tyre Form of tyre construction in which the wraps of fabric in the tyre carcass are laid over each other diagonally instead of radially (see radial ply).

Cush drive A shock-absorbing component in a transmission system.

Cylinder head Component closing the blind end of the cylinder. Houses the valve gear on a four-stroke engine.

D

Damper A device for controlling and perhaps eliminating unwanted movement in suspension systems.

Detonation Explosion of the mixture in the combustion chamber, instead of controlled burning. May cause a tinkling noise, known as pinking, under an open throttle.

Diaphragm The rubber membrane in a master cylinder or carburettor which seals the upper chamber.

Disc brake A brake design incorporating a rotating disc onto which the brake pads are squeezed.

Displacement The amount of volume displaced by the piston of an engine on rising from its lowest position to its highest.

Double-overhead camshaft (DOHC) An engine that uses two overhead camshafts, one for the intake valves and one for the exhaust valves.

Downdraught Downward inclination of the induction tract, usually the carburettor too.

Dry sump Four-stroke lubrication system in which the oil is carried in a separate oil tank and not in the sump.

E

Earth Usually the negative terminal of a battery, or part of the earth return.

Earth return The path of an electrical circuit that returns to the battery, utilising the motorcycle's frame.

ECU (Electronic Control Unit) A computer which controls (for instance) an ignition system, or an anti-lock braking system.

EMS (Engine Management System) A computer controlled system which manages the fuel injection and the ignition systems.

Expansion chamber Section of two-stroke engine exhaust system so designed to improve engine efficiency and boost power.

F

Final drive Description of the drive from the transmission to the rear wheel. Usually by belt on a scooter.

Firing order The order in which the engine's cylinders fire on a multi, or deliver their power strokes, beginning with the number one cylinder.

Flat twin An engine with horizontal adjacent or opposed cylinders, thereby having a flat configuration.

Float A buoyant object. Used in a carburettor to open and close the fuel inlet valve to maintain a constant fuel level.

Float chamber A carburettor component used to stabilise the fuel level in the carb.

Float level The height at which the float is positioned in the float chamber, so determining the fuel level.

Flywheel A rotating mass of considerable weight and radius, used to smooth out power impulses at the crank.

Four-stroke An operating cycle for an internal combustion engine in which combustion takes place on every other ascent of the piston. See also Two-stroke.

Freeplay The amount of travel before any action takes place, for example, the distance the rear brake lever moves before the rear brake is actuated.

Friction The resistance between two bodies moving in contact with each other and relatively to each other.

Front fork Telescopic tubes incorporating springs and dampers used to provide a suspension system for the front of a motorcycle.

Fuel injection The fuel/air mixture is metered electronically and directed into the engine intake ports (indirect injection) or into the cylinders (direct injection). Sensors supply information on engine speed and conditions.

Fuel/air mixture The charge of fuel and air going into the engine.

Fuel level The level of fuel in a float chamber. Can be altered by changing the float level.

Fulcrum The point about which a leverage system pivots.

Fuse An electrical device which protects a circuit against accidental overload.

G

Gasket Any thin, soft material – usually cork, cardboard, asbestos or soft metal – installed between two metal surfaces to ensure a good seal.

Gear A component, often circular, with projections for the positive transmission of movement to a companion gear which may, or may not be, of the same shape and size.

Gearbox An assembly containing the transmission components used in varying the ratio of the gearing.

Gear ratio The ratio of turning speeds of any pair of gears or sprockets, derived from their number of teeth.

Gudgeon pin The pin, usually made of hardened steel, linking the piston to the small end of the connecting rod.

H

HT High Tension Description of the electrical circuit from the secondary winding of the ignition coil to the spark plug.

HT lead A heavily insulated wire carrying the high tension current from the coil to the spark plug.

Horizontally-opposed A type of engine in which the cylinders are opposite to each other with the crankshaft in between.

Hub The centre part of a wheel.

Hydraulic A liquid-filled system used to transmit pressure from one component to another. Common uses on motorcycles are brake and clutch actuating mechanisms.

Hygroscopic Water absorbing. In scooter applications, braking efficiency will be reduced if hydraulic fluid absorbs water from the air – care must be taken to keep new brake fluid in tightly sealed containers.

Hypoid oil An extreme-pressure oil formulated to stand up to severe and unique conditions in hypoid transmission gears.

I

lbf ft Pounds-force feet. An imperial unit of torque. Sometimes written as ft-lbs.

Ignition advance Means of increasing the timing of the spark at higher engine speeds. Done by mechanical means on early engines or electronically by the ignition control unit on later engines.

Ignition timing The moment at which the spark plug fires, expressed in the number of crankshaft degrees before the piston reaches the top of its stroke, or in the number of millimetres before the piston reaches the top of its stroke.

Injector Equipment for squirting a fluid. Used for both fuel and oil.

Inverted forks (upside down forks) The sliders or lower legs are held in the yokes and the fork tubes or stanchions are connected to the wheel axle (spindle). Less unsprung weight and stiffer construction than conventional forks.

J

Jet A hole through which air, fuel or oil passes, the size of the jet determining the quantity.

Joule The unit of electrical energy.

K

Kickstart A crank, operated by foot, for starting an engine.

Knock Similar to detonation, with same end results, but only the end gases in the far reaches of the combustion chamber ignite. The knocking sound, also known as pinking, occurs when the central and outer flame fronts meet.

L

Lambda (l) sensor A sensor fitted in the exhaust system to measure the exhaust gas oxygen content (excess air factor).

Land The raised portion between two grooves (e.g. between the ring grooves in a piston).

Leading link A form of front suspension using a pivoting link – approximately horizontal – with the axle in front of the pivot.

LT Low Tension Description of the electrical circuit from the power supply to the primary winding of the ignition coil.

Lubricant A substance, usually an oil, interposed between rubbing surfaces to decrease friction.

M

Main bearing The principal bearing(s) on which a component is carried but usually reserved exclusively for the crankshaft.

Mainshaft A principal shaft, as in an engine or a gearbox.

Master cylinder The operator end of an hydraulic control system.

Monoshock A single suspension unit linking the swingarm or suspension linkage to the frame.

Multigrade oil Having a wide viscosity range (e.g. 10W40). The viscosity ranges from SAE10 when cold to SAE40 when hot.

Multi-rate A spring which changes length unequally for equal increments of load. (Contrast with constant rate and progressive rate.)

N

Needle roller bearing A bearing made up of many small diameter rollers of hardened steel, usually kept separated by a cage. Often used where lubrication is poor.

Negative earth Using the negative or minus pole of the battery as the earth.

Nm Newton metres used to measure torque.

O

Odometer A mileage recorder.

Oil injection A system of two-stroke engine lubrication where oil is pump-fed to the engine in accordance with throttle position.

Oil pump A mechanically-driven device for distributing oil around a four-stroke engine or pumping oil into a two-stroke engine.

Overhead valve (OHV) A four-stroke engine with the valves in the cylinder head and operated by pushrods.

Overhead cam (OHC) As above but with the camshaft contained in the cylinder head and operated by chain, gear or belt from the crankshaft.

P

Pinking The noise arising from Detonation and Knock.

Plug cap A cover over the top of a spark plug that transmits the HT voltage from the coil and lead to the plug.

Plug lead A heavily insulated wire carrying the high tension current from the coil to the spark plug.

Port Strictly, a hole or opening but also used to described the transfer ports in a two-stroke engine.

Power band The band of rpm in which the engine produces really useful power.

Pre-ignition Auto-ignition taking place before the desired moment and happening, not by sparking, but by incandescence.

Pre-load (suspension) The amount a spring is compressed when in the unloaded state. Pre-load can be adjusted by gas, spacer or mechanical adjuster. Determines ride height.

Premix The method of engine lubrication on older two-stroke engines. Engine oil is mixed with the petrol in the fuel tank in a specific ratio.

Primary gears The pair of gears connecting the crankshaft to the clutch in a unit construction engine.

Progressive rate A spring that progressively deflects less for equal increments in load (see Constant rate and Multi-rate).

Pushrod A stout rod used to transmit a push as in clutch or overhead-valve operation.

R

Radial ply tyre Form of tyre construction in which the wraps of fabric in the tyre carcass are laid over each other radially, and not diagonally.

Radiator Device for losing heat.

Rake The angle of the steering axis from the vertical.

Rebore Removing the worn surface of a cylinder to create a new working surface.

Rebound damping A means of controlling the oscillation of a suspension unit spring after it has been compressed.

Rectifier Electrical device passing current in one direction only (and thus a wave), used to convert alternating current into direct current.

Reed valves A valve functioning like a reed, with pressure causing the 'flap' to open or close.

Regulator Device for maintaining the charging voltage from the generator or alternator within a specified range.

Relay An electrical device used to switch heavy current on and off using a low current auxiliary circuit. Relays are used to switch heavy currents such as for the starter motor.

Rim The edge, margin or periphery. In the case of a wheel, the part that carries the tyre.

Rising rate Condition set up using a three-way linkage between the swingarm and the shock absorber to give progressive suspension action.

Roller bearing One containing rollers as the support medium, and not balls.

rpm Revolutions per minute.

S

Seizure The binding together of two moving parts through pressure, temperature or lack of lubrication, and often all three.

Shock absorber A device for ironing out the effects of riding over bumps in the road to give a smooth ride.

Single-overhead camshaft (SOHC) An engine that uses one overhead camshaft to operate both intake valves and exhaust valves via rockers.

Small-end The smaller end on a connecting rod to which the piston is attached.

Spark plug Device for arcing an electric current, as a spark, between two electrodes inserted in the combustion space.

Spindle The fixed rod about which an article turns or perhaps swings in an arc.

Sprocket Toothed wheel used in chain drive.

Stanchion In a telescopic front fork, that tubular part attached to the fork yokes and on or in which travels the moving slider.

Steering head The part of the frame which houses the steering stem.

Stroke The distance between the highest and lowest points of the piston's travel.

Sub-frame The rear part of a motorcycle frame which carries the seat, rear lighting and electrical components.

Sump Chamber on the bottom of a four-stroke engine that contains the oil.

Swingarm Supports the rear wheel and rear suspension.

T

Taper rollerbearing A hardened steel roller, being tapered instead of cylindrical.

Tachometer Rev-counter.

Thermostat Controls the flow of engine coolant into the radiator.

Timing The opening and closing points of valves and the moment of ignition in the engine cycle.

Top Dead Centre (TDC) Highest point of a piston's stroke.

Top-end A description of an engine's cylinder block, head and valve gear components.

Torque A twisting force about a shaft, measured in Nm, kgf m or lbf ft.

Trail The distance between the point where a vertical line through the wheel axle touches the ground, and the point where a line through the steering axis touches the ground.

Twistgrip Rotary throttle control on the right handlebar, operated by twisting.

Two-stroke An operating cycle for an internal combustion engine.

V

Variator A variable pulley that changes a scooter's gearing through centrifugal force as engine speed rises and falls.

Index

accessories 10, 62-63
  performance parts 55
air filters 100, 115
airboxes 100
Aprilia DiTech motor 27, 74-75
Audi TT 25

badge engineering 13, 15
batteries 33, 62-63, 77, 82-83, 85, 93, 134-135, 141
  checking 134
  lead acid 134
  sealed-for-life 134
battery chargers 63, 107
  trickle chargers 63, 134, 141
bearings 132-133, 137, 139-140
big bore kits 100
big-wheeled scooters 30-31
Bimota Tesi motorcycle 18
bodywork 92-93
  removing and refitting panels 93
braking systems 39, 66-67, 90-91, 101, 126-129, 138
  ABS 25, 91, 138
  braided hoses 17
  callipers 127-128
  checking 113, 122, 127, 135, 138
  disc brakes 13, 17, 25, 29, 31, 33, 57, 66, 90-91, 126-128, 138, 141
  drum brakes 13, 23, 25, 31, 33, 90-91, 126-127, 138
  fluids 112, 128-129, 138
  hydraulic 23, 129, 138
  linked brakes 9, 15, 17, 25, 27, 29, 91
  master cylinders 113
  pads 10, 109, 113, 127-128, 138
  shoes 128-129
budget price scooters 15, 21, 25, 31

cables 129-131
carburettors 23, 72-74, 98-99, 115, 119, 121-122, 141
  constant velocity (CV) 73
  slide 72-73
catalytic converters 13, 18, 23, 78-79, 122
circuit breakers 135
cleaning 58, 108-109, 115, 122, 135, 140
  degreasers 109, 123
  jet washers 109
clocks 25
clothing and riding equipment 10, 37, 39, 42-53, 55, 63
  armour 44-45

boots 39, 48-49, 51
Day-Glo vests 63
earplugs 43
footwear 48-49
gloves 39, 43, 46-47, 49, 51, 53, 60-61
goggles 42
high-tech fabrics 47, 49
jackets 39, 44-45, 49, 51, 63
parkas 51
protective 44-47, 49
PVC oversuits 51
reflective material 51, 63
thermals 52-53
trousers 44-45, 49, 53
waterproofing 39, 44-45, 47, 49-51
commuter scooters 13
Compulsory Basic Training (CBT) 37-41
  Form DL196 39
congestion charges 9
cooling systems 116-118, 141
  anti-freeze 112, 116, 141
  coolant pumps 13, 117
  cooling fans 67
  maintenance 116-117
  radiators 13, 116
  thermostats 112
covers 58, 63
crash protection 44-47

dashes 135
dealerships 11, 19
decarbonisation (decoke) 117
derestriction 9, 13, 15, 19, 31, 55, 77, 94-95, 98-99, 101
diagnostic computers 27
Driving Standards Authority (DSA) 40-41
Ducati motorcycles 85

electric scooters 32-33
electrical systems 82-83, 134-135, 140
  alternators 82, 125
  connectors 83, 135
  detecting faults 107
  fuses 83, 135
  sensors 83
  starters 83
  wiring 134-135
  12-volt 82
electronic control units (ECU) 74-75, 100
Elf GP cars 18
emissions
  low/free 15, 33
  regulations 13, 18, 21, 23, 72, 75

two-stroke 18, 69, 75
engines 68-69
   air-cooled 13, 15, 18, 21, 23
   combustion cycles 69-70
   four-strokes 69-70, 125
   liquid-cooled 13, 15, 18, 23, 25, 31, 116, 141
   management systems 83
   two-strokes 70-71, 117
   tuning 18-19, 77, 79, 94-101
   50cc 9, 12-16, 19, 31, 33, 37, 39, 41-42, 55,
      94-101
   75cc 37, 41
   100cc 21, 31
   120cc 41
   125cc 15, 22-23, 27-29, 31, 36-37, 39, 41,
      69
   150cc 28, 31
   175cc 28
   180cc 29
   200cc 27-28
   250cc 28, 74
   400cc 28-29
   500cc 27-29
   650cc 28-29
entry level scooters 12-13
examiners 41
exhaust systems 19, 75, 78-79, 98, 101, 118,
   137
   cleaning and checking 117, 122
   race 19
   silencers 67, 79, 137, 141

fasteners 93, 105, 107
   checking tightness 122, 138-139
filler caps 111-112, 120
footboards and rests 21, 85, 93, 139
frames 25, 29, 84, 124, 139
   aluminium beam 85
   monocoque 85
   spine 85
   steel trellis 85
fuel 11, 141
   unleaded petrol 79, 112
fuel/air mixture 70, 72-79, 100, 121
   Stoichiometric ratio 72
fuel economy 21, 63, 95
fuel injection 18, 25, 27, 31, 74-75, 79, 83
fuel systems 69, 72-75, 119
   filters 119
   hoses (lines) 119, 121
   pumps 119
   reed valves 100

garaging 55, 58, 140-141
grey imports 9,11
grocery hooks 67

heated grips 27-28, 62-63, 83
helmets 28, 39, 42-43, 47, 53, 55
   cleaning 43

European standard 43
   full-face 42-43
   open face 42-43
   storage 57, 60-61
   visors 43
Highway Code 39
Honda motors 21
horns 83, 113, 135-136

ice-warning systems 28
idle speed (tickover) adjustment 121
ignition 76-77 83
   flywheel generators 77
   HT coils 77
   misfire 77
   timing 100
instructors 37, 41
insurance 10-11, 13, 22, 54-56, 101, 131
   comprehensive 54-55
   excess 55
   no claims discount 55
   personal injury claims 55
   third party 54
   third party, fire and theft 54
intercoms 62, 83

kickstarts 83, 141
Kymco engine 23

L-plates 37, 39, 41
licences 36, 39, 41, 55, 94
   A1 36-37, 41
   Direct 37, 41
   Accelerated Access 37, 41
   full car 37, 40
   full motorcycle 26
   moped 37, 41
   penalty points 41
   Provisional 37, 55
   Restricted (A) 36-37, 41
   restrictions 10, 13, 19, 21-22, 101
lighting and signalling systems 10, 13, 61, 66-67,
   83, 121
   brake 135-136
   bulbs 83, 135
   checking 113, 135-136
   courtesy 25, 29
   hazard warning systems 136
   headlights 121, 136
   indicators 61, 66, 83, 135-136
   LED 17
   tail 136
   warning 83

lubrication 123, 125, 132
luggage and storage 23, 25, 28, 49, 51, 60-62,
   99
   bungee cords 61
   gloveboxes 29, 61
   hard luggage 60

lockable compartments 29
    panniers 31, 60
    racks 60-61
    rucksacks 60-61
    soft luggage 60
    top boxes 25, 31, 60
    underseat storage 25, 27, 29, 31, 57, 60-61

maintenance 58, 114-129
Malossi belts 99
mirrors 93
mobile phone sockets 25, 27-29
Mods 51
mopeds 31, 36-37, 39-40, 47
Morini motor 31
MoT test 136-137

noise regulations 79, 137
number plates 10

oil 11, 111, 141
    changing 120
    checking 119-120
    damping 138
    drain and filler plugs 118, 120, 122
    engine 118, 125
    filters 118
    gearbox 120
    two-stroke 111, 115, 117
on-the-road charges (OTR) 10
Oxford Products 61, 63

paint schemes 15, 17, 21, 28
parallel imports 10-11
parking 8, 57-58
parts (genuine and pattern) 11
Piaggio motors 31
    Hi-Per Pro 2 18
    Leader 23, 25, 68
pillion passengers 27, 37, 41, 61-62, 99, 121
    seat 67
pre-ride checks 110-111
    coolant 112
    fuel 112
    oil level 111

radiator sealants 116
radio cassette players 23, 27
retro style 9, 11, 15, 23, 31
rev counters (tachometer) 27, 121
riding tests 36-41
    Direct/Accelerated Access 36
    eye sight 39, 41
    hazard perception 40
    theory 37, 40-41
road tax (disc) 10-11, 54, 136
roll cages 28
Rotax engine 31
running costs 11

security 15, 56-59
    alarms 55, 57, 59, 83, 141
    anti-theft precautions 55
    Boa locks 15, 19, 21, 31
    ground anchors 58
    immobilisers 15, 19, 21, 25, 31, 55, 57, 59, 83
    ignition key security 57
    insurance conditions 54
    locks 55, 57
    marking systems 55, 59
    steering locks 57
    U-locks 57
service intervals 114, 129
spark plugs 69, 71, 75, 77, 121-122, 125, 141
    cleaning 122
speedometers 17, 66, 123
spoilers 21
sports scooters 9, 13, 16-19, 31, 75, 95
stands 67, 123
    checking 113, 122
    electric 28
    getting bike on and off 39
steering 137, 140
    bearings 133, 137
    checking 113
    hub-centre 18
super scooters 26-29, 84, 98
suspension 15, 18, 66, 88-89, 124, 132-133,
    138, 140-141
    checking 113, 122, 124, 138
    leading link 89
    monoshock front 124
    Paioli shocks 15
    right way up (RWU) forks 88
    shock absorbers 25, 67, 89, 96, 99, 109, 121,
    138
    Showa forks 25
    springs 89
    swingarms 18, 29, 85, 89, 109, 122, 132-133,
    138
    telescopic forks 18, 88, 124
    trailing links 88-89
    upside-down (USD) forks 17, 88

tanks (fuel and oil) 85, 119, 121, 141
temperature gauges 112
throttles 9, 39, 66, 72-73, 81, 113, 121, 137
tools 104-107
    Allen keys 106
    pliers 107
    screwdrivers 106
    socket sets 106
    spanners 105
    torque wrenches 107, 120, 122
Toyota F1 colours 17
training 10
    schools 37, 39
transmission systems 67, 80-81, 95-96, 120, 137
    automatic 29, 36, 80-81, 121
    bearings 132

checking drain plugs 122
clutches 2339, 97-98, 125
drive belts 117
filters 115
gear levers 39
lubrication 120
manual gearboxes 23, 36, 80-81
pulleys 96, 98, 117, 125
variators 97-98, 100, 125
   Omega Racing 98
trip computers 28
twistgrips 9, 72-73, 80, 121
tyres 10-11, 23, 31, 86-87, 99, 139
bias-belted 87
checking 113, 125, 139, 141
Continental Zippy 2 99
cross-ply 87
direction arrows 87, 113, 139
low-profile 15, 17
pressure gauge 62-63, 113
punctures 87
radial 87
running-in 87
tread wear indicators (TWI) 87, 113
tubeless 87
valve caps 87, 112, 125
valves 87

valve clearances, checking 125

warranty conditions 11, 13
weather protection 25, 27-28, 50
front screens 28, 42, 50
leg shields 29, 50, 60, 85, 92
roofs 28, 50, 92
rear screens 28
wheels 31, 84
alignment 139
balancing 87
bearings 132, 139-140
cast alloy 87, 125, 139
checking 122, 125, 139
large 17, 25, 30-31
pressed steel 87
spare 23
Williams BMW F1 28

Yamaha
GTS1000 motorcycle 18
Minarelli motor 25

Scooter makers and models
Adly 12-13, 21
Predator II 17
Aprilia 17-18
Atlantic 125 23
Atlantic 200 9, 27
Atlantic 500 26-27
Drag 9

Habana 23
Leonardo ST 25
Mojito Custom 15, 23
Scarabeo 50 9, 31
Scarabeo 100 31
Scarabeo 125GT 31
SR50 13, 75
SR50 DiTech 13, 19
Bajaj Classic SL125 23
Barrus Wasp 13
Benelli 17, 19, 25
Adiva 125 23, 50, 92
Adiva 150 28, 50, 92
K2 Air 31
K2 100 21
Pepe LX 50 31
491 RR 17
Beta 23
Eikon 50 15
Eikon 125 25
BMW
C1 28, 50, 92
200 Executive 28
Branson 25
CPI 12-13
Derbi 17
Atlantis 13
Atlantis 100 21
Fosti 25
Gilera 18
DNA 85
Nexus 29
Runner VX 125 25
Stalker 13
Her Chee 13
Honda 21, 57
Dylan 25
Lead SCV100 21
Pantheon FES 25
SGX50 Sky 31
SH50 31, 37
SH125 31
SFX 15
Silverwing 29
Vision 13
X8R 15
X8R-S 17
X8R-X 17
Hyosung 12, 21
EZ-100 21
SF50 13
SF50R 17
Italjet 13, 17
Dragster 18, 85
Formula 50 17-18
Formula 50LC 18
Jet Set 23, 25
Millennium 25
Torpedo 50 2T 31
Torpedo 50 4T 31

Torpedo 125 31
Kangda 25
  ZS125T-3 25
  ZS125T-4 25
  ZS125T7 25
  ZS125T9 25
Kymco 12, 25
  Ego 125 25
  Miller 125 25
  Movie XL125 25
  Super 9 13
LML Star Deluxe 125 23
Malaguti 17
  Madison 400 28-29
  Phantom 100 D 21
MBK 15, 17, 25
  Doodo 125 25
  Ovetto 15
  Skyliner 25
  Stunt 50 19
  Thunder 125 25
Moto-Roma 13, 25
  GrandPrix 50 17
Peugeot 15, 17-19, 25, 57
  Elyseo 100P 21
  Elystar 15
  Elystar Advantage 25
  Elystar 125P 25
  Jet Force 50 SBC 17, 85
  Jet Force 125 25, 85
  Lepton E 33
  Looxor 50 31
  Looxor 50 TDSi 31
  Looxor 125 31
  Looxor 150 SBC 31
  Metal X2 19
  Scoot'elec 33
  Speed 100 21
  Speedfight Furious 19
  Speedfight WRC 206 21
  Speedfight X-Race 21
  Speedfight 2X 18
  Speedfight 2XP 18
  Vivacity 100 NP 21
  VSX 100P 21

Piaggio 15, 18, 23, 57
  B125 31
  B500 27
  Liberty 50 31
  Skipper 25
  X9 125 Evolution 23
  X9 500 27
  X9 500 SL 27
  Zip SP 18
  Zip 125 23
ScootElectric
  Magic 33
  Oxygen 33
  Raider 45 33
  SWAP 33
Suzuki 57
  AY50 Katana 17
  Burgman 400 29
  Burgman 650 28-29
Sym 21, 25
  Euro MX125 25
  Jet Euro X100 21
  Joyride 25
  Megalo 25
  Shark 25
Vespa 23, 85
  ET2 15
  ET4 15, 23-25
  Granturismo 24
  GT125 23
  PX125 22-23, 36
Yamaha 17, 25
  B Whizz 95, 98
  Jog R 15
  Jog RR 14-15
  Majesty 125 24-25, 29, 61
  Majesty 180 29
  Majesty 400 29
  Maxster 25
  VP300 Versity 29
  XP500 TMax 29
  YN 50 Neos 15
  YQ50 Aerox 17
  YQ100 Aerox 21
Zhongyu CommutaScoota 50 13

Author Acknowledgements:
Bob Gray
Bruce Dunn
Lisa and Esme
Mark Hughes
Simon Larkin
Louise McIntyre,
Simon Larkin,
Hugo Wilson

Written by
Alan Seeley
Design
Simon Larkin
Technical editor
Phil Mather
Editor
Jeff Porter
Project Manager
Louise McIntyre